THE COURAGE TO CHANGE
A Teen Survival Guide

National Library of Canada Cataloguing in Publication Data

Main entry under title:

The courage to change : a teen survival guide

ISBN 1-896764-41-X

1. Violence in adolescence--Canada--Prevention. 2. Violence in adolescence--
Pictorial works. 3. Juvenile delinquency--Canada--Prevention. I. Zosky Proulx, Brenda II.
Leave Out ViolencE (Association)

HV9069.C68 2001   364.4'0835'0971   C2001-901854-1

Book design and layout by Stephanie Martin
Cover photographs by – from left to right, top:
Maureen Rodriguez Labreche; Joy Futerman; Joel Silverstein
Bottom: Maureen Rodriguez Labreche; Maureen Rodriguez Labreche; Beth; Patricia

Printed and bound in Canada
ISBN 1-896764-41-X

Second Printing

Second Story Press gratefully acknowledges the support of the Ontario Arts Council and the Canada Council for the Arts
for our publishing program. We acknowledge the financial support of the Government of Canada through
the Book Publishing Industry Development Program.

Published by
SECOND STORY PRESS
720 Bathurst Street, Suite 301
Toronto, ON
M5S 2R4
www.secondstorypress.on.ca

THE COURAGE TO CHANGE

A Teen Survival Guide

by the
Leave Out ViolencE Youth

Compiled by
Brenda Zosky Proulx

Second
Story
Press

This book is dedicated to the memory of Daniel Rudberg.
It is also dedicated to the youth of the world
who have the courage to speak out and thus bring positive change
into their own lives and the lives of others.

TABLE OF CONTENTS

The stories and poems in *The Courage to Change: A Teen Survival Guide* are written by remarkable people. In these pages, youth speak with great honesty about the ruinous effect of violence in their lives. They also speak with hope and courage.

Reading about their experiences, we wonder at the ability of the human spirit to endure hardship. But these young people did more than survive. They rejected brutality and used their deep understanding of suffering to become wiser and more compassionate.

In the Synoptic Gospel according to St. Thomas, there is a profound statement about human nature, "If you find out what is within you and you bring out what is within you, what is within you will save you; if you find out what is within you and you do not bring out what is within you, what is within you will destroy you."

This guide for teenagers is all about believing in the possibility for change and finding your real inner self. Every young person whose story appears here has struggled, but they have also persevered. Their determination to learn from the past shows the path to true growth and well-being.

I hope that everyone who reads *The Courage to Change: A Teen Survival Guide* will dedicate themselves to finding personal peace and bringing it to others. I send my warmest congratulations to its contributors and my best wishes to its readers.

Adrienne Clarkson

PREFACE

TWENTY-NINE YEARS AGO, in an act of random senseless violence, Twinkle Rudberg lost her husband, Daniel, to the anger of a fourteen-year-old boy. Daniel Rudberg intervened in a purse-snatching incident in Montreal and died instantly from stab wounds. The incident changed Twinkle Rudberg's life. While initially dealing with her own feelings of being victimized, she eventually recognized that the boy was a victim as well. In 1993, she founded Leave Out ViolencE (L.O.V.E.).

THIS BOOK IS ABOUT COURAGE, change and survival, words which have been key in my life. In order to survive, I had to find courage within myself. Leave Out ViolencE was founded because of the path I chose in answer to the greatest challenge of my life. The choices that have affected my life have been dramatic. They started many years ago when my parents were looking for a child to adopt and I was their choice. How fortunate I was; I grew up privileged and life for me was happy and fulfilling. I was married to a beautiful man, Daniel, with whom I shared a wonderful family. He absolutely loved life.

Then one Saturday night in September of 1972, he made a choice that affected many lives forever. None of us believe that violence will ever touch our lives. Someone else, yes. Me? No! It never entered my mind until that Saturday evening. We were on our way out to dinner with friends when we noticed an elderly lady being attacked by a teenage boy. Daniel went to the aid of the woman and then chased the fourteen-year-old boy and cornered him in some bushes. The boy had a knife and stabbed Daniel to death.

I thought my life had ended along with Daniel's. After many years I came to realize that I had a choice to make. I could be continuously angry, bitter and vindictive; I could give up. Instead, I chose life. I began to look at the life of the boy who had killed Daniel, and became aware that he had been a victim as well. He was often alone and isolated, and had become involved with a gang, with drugs, and with violence. I grew increasingly aware of the proliferation of youth violence and I knew that I wanted to do something to change this alarming trend. I wanted to hear what youth had to say, and to know why their culture was so focused on violence. I wanted to give them a voice.

Once that decision was made, magic happened. I gathered a group of concerned citizens and we decided to go out on a limb and do something for the youth of our society. We realized that we are all responsible for the future of Canada's children. It was because of the nature of Dan's death and the triumph of positive choice that the Leave Out ViolencE organization was started in 1993.

The youth that I have had the great privilege to work with and speak to across Canada inevitably ask me if I feel that Dan's death was predestined. Though I can't answer that, what I do tell them is that a path was put in front of me and I chose to follow it. When we choose life, when we choose to help others, we risk failure, and sometimes we do falter. But every time we bring someone into the light, it affects all of us. I feel deeply blessed to be doing this work. I thank every young person who has touched my life; they make my heart smile. I have huge admiration for their courage to change and their ability to survive the challenges put in their paths. Bravo to all of them!

Twinkle Rudberg
President and Founder of L.O.V.E

INTRODUCTION

THE YOUTH who produced this relentlessly honest book are part of an exciting adventure in social change. They are teenagers who have decided to reject violence by lifting their lives to a higher ground. Now they are helping others to do the same. Their straight-from-the-gut writing and photographs, plus their own hard-won insights, are the tools they use for personal, and then social, change.

First, the teenage authors examined the troubling issues that brought conflict into their lives — family stress, lack of self-esteem, drug abuse. Then they looked for positive, creative solutions. In the process, most found themselves wanting to draw a line in the sand and say no. No more using violence — physical, verbal or emotional — against themselves or others to solve problems. The cycle of violence must be broken. It does not work.

Leave Out ViolencE (L.O.V.E.) is the grassroots organization that underwrites this unique process of social change. The first L.O.V.E. program began in 1995 in the basement photo labs of Montreal's Dawson College with fifteen teens who had experienced violence. To date, approximately 10,000 children and youth have been exposed to its programs across Canada.

L.O.V.E. seeks to stop youth violence, targeting both the individual at risk and the community at large. Through L.O.V.E.'s programs in local colleges or in their own schools, teens who have been perpetrators and/or victims, or witnesses of violence (including assault, substance abuse, bullying, self-mutilation, domestic violence) are given access to the skills, support and sense of purpose they need to reject violent behaviour. In the process they build self-esteem and a sense of community.

L.O.V.E. fosters cultural change in the community by training these young people to become skilled teachers of nonviolence, and to recruit and educate other youths, thereby expanding the movement of nonviolent youth activists across cultural and racial boundaries. Our youth go out into the community and use their multi-media tools to promote nonviolence in schools and community groups, as well as to conferences and youth organizations. They speak about their own experiences and lead discussions on violence prevention. What truly makes L.O.V.E. a dynamic and powerful organization is that the youth who were once the victims and perpetrators are now the people at the forefront advocating change to their peers and the broader community.

Finally, they produce a biannual newspaper, *One L.O.V.E.*, and an exhibit which tours public and private buildings across Canada. Their first book, *L.O.V.E. Works!*, was published by Stoddart in 1998. In 2001, they will begin to do TV broadcasting as well.

L.O.V.E. allows our youth to transcend barriers and change people's perceptions. In doing so, they change the course of their own lives. The skills they gain in literacy, critical thinking, public speaking, group dynamics, technology, leadership and community-building are in turn used to help thousands of other children that conventional methods just don't reach.

The message transmitted through all of our programs is clear: violence, no matter what the media and others say, is not cool. Appreciating your own unique qualities, doing what you love to do, and helping to improve society along the way, however, is super-cool indeed.

Brenda Zosky Proulx
Co-founder of the L.O.V.E. Project

Chapter 1
Feelings

Getting past the confusing, sometimes clashing feelings of anger, loneliness and frustration that we live with can seem impossible. Very often we think that we will drown. Our writers in this chapter express both their hope and their despair.

DO YOU HEAR ME?

Laura, 15

Do you hear me?
I need to know;
I am going to go mad.
Listen, listen, please;
help me.
I sit here crying
for your help,
but do you hear me?
Because I really need
to know.

Amber

Anonymous, 16

I never remember what my fights
are about. They just start and
stop the way the sun rises and
sets.

Vicki, 14

Sometimes I cry for nothing.
Well, it must be for something; I just don't know
what.

Kym, 17

I fought with him, I swore at him, but I never spoke to him.
I never asked him why. Maybe it would have saved me the
guilt and the hatred towards him afterwards. I can't change
the past; I can only change the future. I'm tired of being
angry all the time.

BREAKING DOWN THE WALL

Andrew, 16

I build a wall
around me, I lay
it brick by brick until
it passes my head.
Help me break the wall
so I can be free of myself;
help me understand myself,
help me to live.

Patricia

INSTEAD OF JUST running away from your problems either by burning a spliff or jugging a forty down, use other options. Build your courage; believe in yourself.

In Search of the Spark

Amber, 16

I am lost. I wander. I do not belong. I am the lone wolf
with frost patterns in my eyes.
I don't deserve to be seen. I don't deserve warmth;
       smiles are my armour, laughter my shield
Look hard and you might find what I have hidden:
       Black flames that lick my bones
       Soot that chokes me
       Ashes that sting my eyes
       Grey smoke of evil, I fear will creep out
       A lifeless skeleton, brittle, haunted with sin.
But maybe somewhere inside is a tiny light.
A solitary flicker. A spark, a glow of courage and hope
That can be lit by love and forgiveness
That can explode into a burst of goodness
And smoulder the black.

Before you get mad, think about things you
can do to relieve yourself of the anger and
then, when you do get mad, try them out.

Sandra, 14

Past experiences of my life scared me, completely corrupting my mind and destroying my emotions. **Violence has played a huge part in my life.** Sometimes violence feels like the only way to get out your anger and frustration. You feel like you're in a dark never-ending hole. But then you help yourself climb up; **you use other options to solve your problems** instead of just running away from them by either burning a spliff or jugging a forty down. **You build your courage**; believe in yourself. And once you accomplish these things, a light will come to you, because you'll have climbed up out of the hole and into a better future.

Try to find out what the rage inside of you is about, what the root of it is.

Kym, 17

Little girl — one of the most innocent things you can be. Now, as a teen, **my heart and soul are full of anger and confusion.** I hear myself yelling and punching. I fall to my knees, my body shaking as if a big heat wave was running through my body.

Once a child who had faith, hope and a dream; now the monster in the closet or under the bed, crushing the little girl dreams that I once had.

Jessica, 16

Dear Adult World,

You always complain about teenagers crowding your streets, shopping centres and parks. But **where are we to go?** Everything is yours, and nothing is ours — unless, of course, it costs money. Anything that I want to do costs money, but money is something I never have. **I want some place to call my own,** where me and my friends can stay for more than ten minutes without having to dodge security guards. And I wish that place were somewhere where what teens need was actually taken into consideration when it was being set up.

Anonymous

I just wish that for once adults took notice of how few options they've created for us, and finally took the responsibility to do something for our sake.

Andrew, 16

Try to find out what the rage inside of you is about, what the root of it is. Sit down by yourself or with someone you trust and have a conversation.

To control one's rage is an art form. **Before you get mad,** think about things you can do to relieve yourself of the anger and then when you do get mad, try them out. Things that might work are: **reading, writing, jogging, lifting weights, talking,** sitting down, listening to music, breaking sticks outside to prevent yourself from breaking things.

We need to find that child in ourselves, to help keep that child alive in others and to share that goodness.

You have to understand that **change will not happen overnight.** It's a long and tiresome process. You literally pick apart your own psyche to try and understand yourself and the world around you better, because **the world around you affects you.** You have to release the constraints that are holding you back from understanding yourself.

And always remember that **you are not the only person going through this**, there are many others.

How I Stopped Hating

Amber, 16

I once had the privilege of holding a newborn baby in my arms. I was fascinated by how this little one could be **so perfect and pure**. This baby could not be anything *but* goodness and innocence in a blanket.

Later, when I was confronted by a person I hated, I looked at him, at his eyes, nose, lips; looked at the way he moved and spoke.

And then I imagined what he must have looked like as a newborn baby. I pictured him with tiny fingers curled into little fists. **I imagined him with little feet and kicking legs,** chubby tummy and delicate lips, soft plush skin and beautiful, trusting blue eyes. I smelled that fresh

baby smell, heard the little noises, felt the fuzzy hair on his head. I looked back at the grown person and **my hate melted away.**

Then I felt a bit sad. Sad that this person, who once was a small bundle of joy, had seen too much of the darkness in the world and had grown up with a lot of pain and anger. **I was sorry for this person,** I prayed that he would one day find that soft little baby in himself: the little baby with eyes of innocence and little belly who only needed love and hugs to thrive, who gave only love and goodness (and dirty diapers) to all those who laid eyes on him.

We were all newborns once. All bundles of joy and innocence. Sadly, some people tend to lose a lot of that. We just need to

find that child in ourselves,

to help keep that child alive in others and to share that goodness. So I hope the next time you feel hate towards someone, you will **picture him or her as a baby,** and your hate will leave you. We need to stop hating.

You can't change the past; you can only change the future.

Chapter 2
Self-Image

It's not always easy to accept what we see in the mirror. Sometimes our attempts to shatter these images are as devastating as the images themselves. Here the powerful voices of our writers discover the ways and means to take apart the destructive patterns and uncover new ways of seeing.

SATISFIED

Morgan, 18

she stands
four-inch heels
before full-length mirror,
faded pictures creased into its corners
she stares
as blunt eyes drown
in thick skin's layers of Cover Girl

nails glisten
trembling hands press against
tiny bulimic bulge
this season's hottest hairstyle sizzles
around her masked face

where a strained gaze
touches snapshots of an exuberant child
she knows
    she smiles
pleased at the new and improved self
Ms Popularity, Tae-bo Queen, quarterback's dream

GIRL TOUGH

GIRL TOUGH

Alexia, 17

GIRLS ARE DEFINITELY CRACKING MORE HEADS THAN THEY USED TO. Some girls think they have to. **We live in a male-dominated society** and girls have to compete with the big boys, even if that means doubling the body count.

Theories about girl violence abound, but I think **we've bought into the image** supplied to us by advertising, film and television: Tough girls are cool. Tough girls are sexy. Tough girls are ready to scrap and kick some shit.

Maureen Rodriguez Labreche

We're not supposed to let people walk all over us. But no one told us how. We never learned that being assertive doesn't necessarily mean being violent. So we went the way shown to us by the media, the way that gets attention, reaction and results.

We should be strong and we shouldn't let people walk all over us or treat us badly, but we need to be taught a new way to be assertive. **I don't want to be violent.** I just want to be able to stand up for myself in an effective way, in a way that people will respond to. Give me a voice so I don't need to use my physical strength.

Strength is new for girls; power is new for girls. Girls have learned they can use violence to gain power. **Power can be a nice feeling**. Feeling strong is a nice feeling. **Just give me a better way to feel it.**

Tiffany A., 19

I really don't mind being called a freak. To me, it's a compliment, because everyone is different. I try to be myself, and when someone calls me a freak, I know I have achieved that.

Stacy, 17

I think respect is one of the most important rules to live by. **If you respect yourself and others, they'll respect you.** This in turn means that they won't do anything to harm you, or make you go against your beliefs.

Amber, 16

Beauty is the heat from the sparks that burn in our soul.

Anonymous, 15

I used to think I was all hard-core and rugged, until one day **that attitude hit me like a rock** and turned my life around for the better.

It was a Friday afternoon, a typical day for me, going to school acting like I was the star of the school. **I made a decision that day that could have changed my life forever.**

I went for a walk in East Vancouver with my classmate, John. We came up to this car and John asked me how I liked it. He told me that it was his friend's car and that his friend had lent it to him. **So, not thinking, I immediately hopped in the car.** It was not until we started driving that John told me that the vehicle was stolen. And of course I thought it was cool to be riding in a stolen car. John reassured me that we wouldn't get caught.

> WHY WOULD YOU WANT TO CHANGE your body and self to fit in, when everybody is different? That's what makes the world great.

We were driving on the side streets of East Vancouver at a speed of eighty kilometres per hour, which scared me to death. About fifteen minutes later, **I suddenly spotted the police following us.** I told John to pull over, but he didn't listen.

John sped off and parked the car on a street beside a park. We'd both hopped out when this guy walked up and asked us for the location of the nearest Taco Time. Then all of a sudden, I heard, "Vancouver Police." **The next thing I knew, I went flying face first right into the ground.** It turned out the guy had tricked us; he was an undercover cop.

I was trying to turn over to face the ground and one of the police officers thought I was resisting arrest, so **he punched me in the ribs twice,** shoved my face into the mud, and threw a yellow tarp over my body so nobody would recognize me.

After that I was handcuffed and strip-searched. After lying in the cold wet grass for about twenty minutes, both **John and I were thrown in the paddy wagon**. It took us about another twenty minutes to drive down to the police station. We were met by a male and female detective.

It scared me so much that it sent chills down my spine. They took my mug-shot and put it in a file. **They called my foster mom. I felt so stupid.**

While I was waiting for my foster mom, John got his picture taken and they took his fingerprints. Finally, my foster mom came and picked me up. **I was lucky. My charges were dropped** because I was only an accessory and plus it was my first offense.

I have learned a lesson from this incident and **John has learned nothing at all.** Now, I realize I could have been charged and gone to jail and it could have changed my life forever. **Being hard-core and rugged is not really what it's made out to be.**

Gabrielle

KIDS THINK VIOLENCE is cool because they see people that they admire and look up to — actors on TV or family members —acting violent. Also, kids think that if you fight, you are "tough" and "strong," so kids do it to show their strength. If the message were that **staying away from violence takes a lot more strength** and courage, then we might see less violence.

Colleen

I THINK RESPECT is one of the most important rules to live by. If you respect yourself and others, they'll respect you.

Pat's Story

Pat, now fifteen, talks about the period when he hung around with a group called "the cutters" who took out their frustrations by mutilating themselves, cutting through their own flesh with razor blades and knives.

L.O.V.E.: Growing up, were you comfortable with yourself?

PAT: Yes, usually, except for things that had to do with girls; that brought me down on myself. I went out with one girl and found out that **my best friend was cheating on me with her.** I felt like I didn't have anything to live for, so I went into my cutting device for a bit, cutting myself just to get it out. Maybe it'll come out by cutting yourself with razor blades, knives.

It's not easy to stop. My old friends kind of got pissed off. **So I started to hang around with another group called the cutters** who picked up razor blades off the ground. My old friends told me I was stupid for doing it… but I had a big connection with this new group, thinking that this was where I belonged.

I was about ten, eleven. I used to do it after school; we'd cut ourselves before we got on the bus, on the bus. We used to cut each other. **No one could tell; we looked fairly normal.** They got scars on their arms so deep, but, see, I was the one that didn't cut myself so deep. Mine aren't too bad; I have a pretty good one, though.

L.O.V.E.: So there was nobody who said, "I wonder what those kids are up to?"

PAT: The bus driver used to ask us what we were doing at the back of the bus. We'd just tell him "nothing."

I would come home with big scars on my arms and blood running down my arms. My parents would ask me what happened and **I would tell them I got into a fight.** And then one day I was home alone, and when my mom and stepfather came back, I was cutting myself. **When they saw me, I dropped the knife.** They asked me what I was doing, and I told them. They asked what the reason was, and we talked about it. I was surprised at how they took it, that they didn't try to ground me; they just talked to me and asked me what was going on. And my old friends called me up and I told them about it too. **It made me feel better, like maybe somebody does care** about me.

> *That's one of the biggest things that a child needs — knowing that their parents do respect them. All you need is communication; you don't need all that other stuff.*

L.O.V.E.: When you look back at it now, what do you feel?

PAT: Disbelief. I just feel like I was stupid; I didn't need to do that, I could've had another way to get out my anger.

L.O.V.E.: Do you know kids who are doing this right now?

PAT: Yes, the same kids I hung around with then. I think **it was my parents' and my other friends' positive reaction that made me stop.**

L.O.V.E.: And when you look at the friends that are continuing, what would you say?

PAT: I would say that **they need more help;** they need someone to take care of them. They get no respect from anybody. Rough family; parents don't care what the kids do. They'd rather watch TV than talk to their kid. Some parents work a couple of jobs; they're never there. **The kids go home to an empty house.** No one to ask how they're doing, how their day was, or how they have been. The parents are never home, because they're too busy caught up in work. There's something else they're doing; **they don't have time to talk to their kids** or do anything important. Parents think the kids would rather have things than have someone talk to them.

L.O.V.E.: And your parents — you were unsure whether or not they were really there for you until they came through. What made you doubt that they were really there for you?

PAT: Well, we never really talked before. I think that it would have been better if we'd really sat down and talked about how our days were and things like that. I would just come home and go up, and "see you guys later; bye." They never asked me questions or anything like that. I felt like maybe they didn't care how my day went or what happened to me.

That's one of the biggest things that a child needs — knowing that **their parents do respect them**. All you need is communication; you don't need all that other stuff.

Maureen Rodriguez Labreche

I Want To Change

Alexia, 17

I want to change
Learn to breathe again
I lost myself to food
I let it eat my life
I want to change
Learn to eat again
I counted calories
I counted snacks
I want to change
Learn to live again
Forget the constant
Obsession
I want to change
Break the pattern
Binge
Purge
Starve
Slowly suicide
I want to change
A day without
Diet pills

Being hard-core and
rugged is not really what
it's made out to be

Laxatives

Diuretics

Slowly dying body

I want to give it back

Restore its breath

Restore its life

Renew its life

The choice used to be simple:

Thin or dead

To be fat was to die

Control and strength

Is thin

Beauty is thin

I forgot life

Life is beauty

Beauty is in survival

Survival is in food

I want to change

Take back my life

Restore a hollow heart

I want to live

I will learn to live.

The real me

Stacey, 17

As I stand in front of my mirror, I look at my face and tell myself that I'm pretty, that it **doesn't matter what other people think**. But as I stand there it crosses my mind, what the hell am I thinking? **Of course I care what other people think;** if I didn't, I wouldn't follow trends. You look at all these magazines, books, stores, people; you watch TV and movies and you say to yourself, "I want that; it's the style now." How can you not?

Look at all the people with eating disorders: **they're killing themselves to fit in with a certain crowd.** But in reality, they'll never think they're good enough to be a part of the "in crowd."

And every girl wants to be a super model: tall, thin, and pretty. Yeah, they think they will be if they spend thousands of dollars on their faces and go on a diet. And **every guy wishes that he was hot,** with a nice body, great hair and a great smile, and then he could get any girl that he wanted.

But why would you want to change your body and self to fit in, when **everybody is different? That's what makes the world great.** So, as I leave my room, I tell myself that I'm perfect just the way I am, and nothing is going to change that.

Andrew

Chapter 3
Home

This chapter shows just how tough the problems at home can be. But it also shows where hope lies: in the protective love for a sister, the harmony of a guitar chord, the companionship of the street, the warmth of a friend's concern.

THE DARK HOUSE

Anonymous, 15

I look at the dark road
that leads to the dark house
and behind the dark doors
is a family that can't speak
a family with dark problems
that only the children know of
and the mother can't see
the pain of the child
that can't speak of the fear
the fear that forces the children to smile,
to laugh, to love
and the dark sky above
that dark house is the only world
they know of
the only world they don't want
the world they don't need
the dark road
that leads to the dark house
with a family that can't speak and
can't sleep in the dark.

Beth, 17

I spend most of my days on the streets. Not because I have to, just because **I like to shrink back and lose myself in a crowd**, nothing but two eyes in a sea of others. I like to watch people. There are six billion people on this planet, each one with a life, a family and friends, with hopes and dreams, thoughts and emotions. Even though there's really only one earth, I think there are six billion.

Valary

My planet earth, my world, stretches for about six miles and a million pages. **My world is the sidewalks downtown,** decades etched into it by dirty feet. My world is an empty park at night with two friends.

My world is stolen clothes, mismatched socks, and boxer shorts with cartoon characters on them. It's my little sister drawing pictures of herself with our dead cat. It's having **spit fights with my little brother** on the front lawn. It's **my mother's gleeful acceptance of what I do**, even if she doesn't understand why I do it. And my father's eventual acceptance of who I am, if only because I'm exactly who I want to be.

My world is **an empty subway heading westbound at one a.m**. It's sitting in a bus shelter, watching rain pound down on the glass. It's broken TVs, old toys left on the curb for the garbage truck, **loud industrial music and the sound of grinding metal.**

Sometimes, I like to go back to my old school, a world that I've almost entirely left behind. The crack of my collarbone when my friends hug me. I like recounting, the sharing of our worlds, which still touch, but no longer revolve around the same point. **I like the suspicious eyes of the vice-principal**, the gleam of the floors, the smell of life but also of emptiness, because no one really wants to be there. Except me. Sometimes, I like to go there.

And sometimes I like to go home. Because at the end of the day, that's where there are the things that remind me that **this isn't just my world**. That to some people, I really am more than just two eyes in a sea of twelve billion.

I'VE FORGIVEN MYSELF for punishing my mother. I just wish she'd forgive herself too.

I Won't Be What You Say I Am, Daddy

Disgusting. Awful. Stupid. Slut. Words he throws at me, descriptions. Believed them. Sometimes I think I'd rather he hit me. Bruises fade, scabs fall off, but every time I look at him, I hear what he's said. **The words vibrate, a taut string** from top to tip, and something rips, tearing a bit more each time. *Disgusting. Awful. Stupid. Slut.* **This is who I am. Becoming more so each day.** I don't want to be a disgusting, awful, stupid, slut. I won't be.

Anonymous, 15

A**s** I sleepily make my way up the creaky stairs with **my cousin snuggled up to me in my arms**, fresh tears drying on her cheeks, I feel anger and hatred burning in me. Country music with dead voices rages on behind me, **my drunken family singing along with scratchy cries.** My head aches from the noise, and my eyes burn from the smoke and useless crying. My throat is dry from shouting over the music, and my cousin is **red-faced from the fury of not being able to kiss her mother goodnight.** The smell of hard liquor, beer, and cigarette smoke lingers behind us like a persistent demon, beckoning me to stay. I sigh deeply and shrug it off.

Emilie

Ever so carefully, I place my cousin in her bed, beside my own. **She lets out a small startled cry**, then drifts off to sleep again. I stand over her murmuring her bedtime ritual. My fists are clenched, and **I grind my teeth in angry annoyance,** because even through the closed door, their horrible "party" can be heard roaring on, with no chance of stopping. I open the window gingerly, afraid of the tiny spiders hiding in the cracks. A **cool wind cruises in and clears the stench out.** I crawl into bed and as I drift off into slumber, I wonder to myself if a gun would make it easier for me to continue my feverish sleep.

Anonymous, 16

I LOVE MY MOM. I really honestly do. **We've been through hard situations and managed to survive.** I forgave her for abandoning me. I forgave her for choosing drugs and men over her own blood. And I've forgiven myself for punishing her. **I just wish she'd forgive herself too.** She keeps running and running. And when she stops, she has to run again. It makes me so sad. Over and over and over again **broken promises, broken trust.** But I'm still there. I'll always be there. But where is she when I'm in need of love and support? No matter what she does to me or herself, I'm there for her. **She causes so much sadness** but I still come back. I'm addicted to a love that kills.

At the end of the day, home is where there are the things that remind me that this isn't just my world. That to some people, I really am more than just two eyes in a sea of twelve billion.

Anonymous, 15

JANUARY and the **long winter months are always depressing** but that year was by far the worst. Money was tight and I was depressed. My whole family was falling apart. My parents were constantly fighting. On top of all this, my brother, who I am close with, would **get drunk and start fights with me.** Everything was messed up. Then out of nowhere, things just started getting better. **I started playing guitar,** I joined a band, and that alone was a huge help. It was an outlet for stress. As I started to act more pleasant around the house, gradually the situation improved.

That's how I changed my life.

Marie-Line

MY LITTLE SISTER ASKED ME to stop being violent. I know I need to have courage to change and that courage comes from, and is for, her.

TOP

Kimberly, 16

Take a moment,

Listen:

Can you hear that? Well?

Can you? Hear it!

Hear me.

Take time from your life

To listen to someone other than yourself.

Know that you are not alone

And others don't have to be because of your negligence.

Realize that your children have no guidance or reassurance.

You have abandoned them in the world you hate.

You have left them to fend for themselves.

I Remember...

I Remember...

Crystal, 15

I REMEMBER the first time I heard that I had a new little sister. The jealousy I felt towards her, how I refused to touch her, **knowing I would fall in love,** knowing I would grow to take care of her. And the time I held her, **the magic that went through me.** I felt it as I watched her grow into a little girl and heard the first words and sounds that came out of her mouth, saw **the first steps she took towards** me. I remember every birthday, every smile, hug and kiss, every tear that she shed, every game we played, and **all the advice she gave me.** I remember the time she asked me to stop being violent. I know **I need to have courage to change** and that courage comes from, and is for, my little sister, Kayla.

I started playing guitar, I joined a band, and that alone was a huge help. It was an outlet for stress.

My Dad Was – Now He's Not

Jonathan, 16

My dad was a drunk
Now he's not
My dad was on drugs
Now he's not
My dad was an asshole
Now he's not
My dad was violent
Now he's not
My dad was a born jailbird
Now he's not
My dad was a child abuser
Now he's not
My dad was a sexist pig
Now he's not

He was, he was, he was, now he's not

Most of all he was a bad father
Now he's not

Chapter 4

Domestic Violence

Shattered dreams and hopes: how do you survive a home filled with violence? By finding the one person who cares, by helping others who have experienced domestic abuse, by talking it out, and, above all, by rejecting violence as a solution.

Bryan, 19

I grew up in a violent household so **I know the terror you feel when someone you love comes after you** wanting to kick the crap out of you. I've seen how alcohol and drug abuse rips apart otherwise loving families. **I've made a personal vow never to strike family or loved ones.** I want to break the cycle of violence that has plagued my family for generations. My wish is that other people follow in my footsteps and end violence between loved ones.

THERE IS STRENGTH in love, and love in strength.

Crystal, 15

People say youth violence is caused by many things, that there's no one reason. Although I read and listen to what they say, **the only thing I really believe is my own story,** the cause of violence in my life. My mom and stepfather f—ked me up. I went through so much that I can't believe I survived. They mentally and physically hurt me, so that was all I learned and really felt; that was all I knew how to do. That and run.

Anonymous, 17

I used to think that it was all my fault that I was physically abused, that I deserved it. **Talking with others helped a lot.** I've learned that it's not my fault or problem and that at this time in my life, I have a lot going for me.

Anonymous, 16

Patricia

VIOLENCE has been a part of my life from the time I was born. I have recently learned to deal with my hurt, frustration and anger without resorting to violence. **What keeps me going is working with my peers,** helping them with their problems; as a result they help me. I wouldn't be here right now if I hadn't realized that **I'm not alone,** that there are other people out there in the same situation.

Strong Arms

Strong Arms

Savannah, 17

I can sit back now and remember the first time I saw my father beat my mother. **I was less than four years old.** I was so scared that I crawled under my parents' bed and cried.

The first time my father hit me, I was four years old. I had used a kitchen knife to cut hearts into the toilet cover. **The next thing I remember was my father's fist coming towards my face,** and how I flew backwards into the bathtub and hit my head on the soap tray.

For almost fifteen years, I lived in a very abusive household. For a while I didn't even want to live any more. **I began to take all my anger and frustration out by cutting myself** with knives or razor blades. I once stabbed the inside of my thigh with a kitchen knife before going to sleep; I threw myself in front of a car, tried to OD on pills one time. There were **so many days when I thought about running away** or moving out, even though I had no place else to go. The hope and dream of one day being set free was all that kept me in the least bit sane. That day did come, sooner than I thought, but not how I'd ever imagined it.

> IF YOUR FATHER OR YOUR MOTHER is beating you, it is because they are cowards.

On March 28, 1998, **my father and I got into a really big fight.**

To this day I don't even know why we started to fight; he just blew up at me.

About half an hour into our scream-fest, my father's voice became very violently aggressive. I could see that **he was about ready to charge me like a bull and beat me down**. Beat down all my feelings, love and self-esteem.

I snapped before my father did. I picked up a huge heavy glass jar, smashed it on his head, and left my house. **I had nowhere to go;** I was just running.

I called home about six or seven hours later and my mother picked up the phone. She was very angry and upset. **My father had gone to the hospital** because I had badly cut his forehead and he had to get stitches. When my mother told me that, **I had no feelings toward the incident.** All my insides were empty. I didn't know what or how to feel, or if I was supposed to feel anything.

On the phone my mother told me that I was mentally ill, **a disgrace to the family,** and that she couldn't stand to see my face. She also said that she had packed a bunch of my stuff, and **called social services.** I was to go to the 29th Avenue Skytrain station as soon as possible. A social worker would pick me up there and put me into a group home. **I'll never forget that journey** to the Skytrain station.

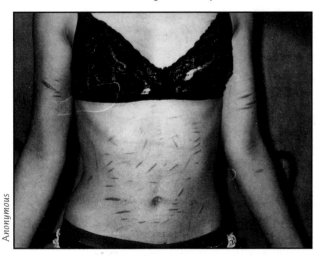

Anonymous

It was cold, windy and raining. I was only wearing a thin shirt, so I was freezing. I stepped in a puddle on the way, so **my socks were soggy and my feet were wet.** The wind was blowing through my hair as I walked towards the park by the Skytrain. I remember thinking, "**What's happening to me?** What kind of place am I moving to? Am I going to be okay?" **I sat down on the tire swing and began to cry.** I was scared, small inside, and alone.

That night I got placed into my first group home.

As soon as I stepped through those doors, **I felt scared, insecure and deathly shy.** I didn't know how to talk to anybody, or voice any opinion. I didn't know I had an opinion, or if it even mattered. **I was like a turtle hiding in a shell** that nobody could crack. I dropped out of school for the six months I lived in that group home. I was anorexic, bulimic and severely depressed.

In the following September, I moved into a foster home and started school again. My foster parents worked a lot, and I was the only child, so **I was very lonely.** I began to miss more and more school, and I hadn't really spoken to anyone in my family for about six months.

I really hated coming home to an empty house, so I moved into another group home. **People really did care about me** in that house, and I got over all of my eating disorders, but I didn't want to care or get close to anybody. When the home became too family-oriented, I moved out again.

The whole idea of a family scared me.

On January 22, 1999, I moved into the house that I am still presently living in. When I moved in, **I was failing school, had no self-esteem,** and still wasn't getting along with my family. I didn't care about myself. In fact, I didn't care about anything. **I started to rely on drugs and alcohol** to get me through my days. I couldn't do anything without them; they were the only comfort I felt I had.

> I'VE MADE A PERSONAL VOW NEVER to strike family or loved ones. I want to break the cycle of violence that has plagued my family for generations.

My foster mother, Jocelyn, could glimpse the true me behind my black wall. **She knew that I was lost,** needed help, guidance and love. She talked to me a lot, and slowly helped me find myself through all the dark clouds. **I stopped abusing my mind and body with drugs and alcohol.** As soon as that happened, I began to feel a lot better about myself. At about the same time, my father checked himself into a four month anger-management program. He realized all the wrong he had done and wanted to change himself. **My father and I were able to start our relationship all over again.**

After I moved in with Jocelyn, **not once did I feel unimportant or stupid.** Jocelyn made sure that I felt important, smart and strong. She never spoke to me like a f—ked up teenager; we talked one on one. **She helped me open my eyes** to strengths, skills and talents that I never knew I had.

I switched schools around early April that year, and began to do well in school again. I realized that **school wasn't that hard if I tried.**

When I brought home **my first straight A report card** in June, I had an ear-to-ear grin all day. I just felt like — "wow"! It's an unforgettable feeling. **I changed my life right around.**

When I think about my life now, I don't think I would have felt that "wow" if it weren't for the house I'm living in and the person who runs it. **I have put Jocelyn through a lot, but she never gave up on me.** She and my boyfriend have been the only people to crack my shell. Jocelyn was the **first person to stand by me** and take me through to the other side. Her strength, security, ideas and love have helped make me the person I am today. I have the utmost admiration for her.

If one person cares, they can truly make a difference, and be a positive influence in many peoples' lives.

There is strength in love, and love in strength.

Patricia

HOME

Anonymous, 17

Shattered dreams
Shattered hope
Shattered glass
Noise rushes louder
And crescendos until I hear
CRASH!
Pain comes
I bleed
Until tomorrow
But what if tomorrow never came
And today stays
Although I feel I'm in a dream
I can't wake up
I can't sleep
I can't feel
I can't fall
All I can do is stand.

Jonathan, 16

I can still remember **the first time that I got beaten by my dad. I was about two years old** and I did something that he didn't like. He hit me, kicked me, punched me, burned me with his cigarettes. He left me with scars on my chest and shoulders from the cigarettes. Not only did he leave me with **scars on the outside;** he also left me with the horrible memories and rage on the inside.

Growing up being abused wasn't the greatest feeling in the world. My family was on welfare; we never had any money. My dad was using the money he had on drugs. When he took drugs he became a horrifying person. He would start to beat me, my brother and my mom.

But believe it or not, **these scars that will haunt me for as long as I live** have helped me as well. When I was in elementary school I would go around every day picking fights with everyone in the school yard. When I reached high school I wised up. **I told myself that I wasn't going to be like my dad.** Although I was living in a group home and not with him, this was easier said than done. It took me four years to finally clean up my act. It was hard but I did it.

I'd like to tell all the young people out there that have this problem not to let it get to you. If your father or your mother is beating you, it is because they are cowards and they are afraid of people their age and they are afraid of doing good things.

This is how I turned my life around. **I joined hockey at the age of ten.** I fell in love with it and plan to make a career out of it. I started to listen in school and not care where my father was or what he was doing. But if you can resolve the conflicts with your father, that's great. But if he hits you again, find a social worker and get yourself put into as foster home. It will work out for the best.

I am now going into grade eleven. I finished grade ten on the Honour Roll. I play inter-city hockey and **I'm known in half of the province for what I can do.**

My advice to all of you children being abused is to **do something with your life**. Stay away from drugs and violence. Stay in school, study hard, and do everything to the best of your abilities. Don't let the abuse bring you down — make it bring you up. Never hit your wife or children, because it is not right. Whenever you feel like hurting someone, think of what I have done. **Talking about my feelings is the hardest thing in the world for me**. The reason I am writing this is to make sure no one ever has to take abuse and go through what I went through.

When you are mad and feel like hurting someone, remember this saying:

"Do unto others as you would have others do unto you."

I STOPPED ABUSING my mind and body with drugs and alcohol. As soon as that happened, I began to feel a lot better about myself.

Anonymous, 16

DEAR MOM,

Mom, I love you and I wish you would love me too. Even though we argue, it doesn't mean my love isn't true. **Sometimes you don't want to understand.** Can you listen to what I have to say instead of ignoring me and going away? **Mom, do you love me?** When I go to bed, I think you don't, because **you always hit me even though you said you wouldn't.** I stay with you because I love you no matter what you do. I don't want to leave you because you because **I don't know where to go** and I still need a mother because I'm only sixteen years old. Sometimes, once or twice every two or three months, you hit me really bad. **It scares me,** because every time you hit me I feel so much pain inside. I know you don't love me. You hit me because you get mad at everything I do. **You think that everything is so bad,** but the truth is I don't do such bad things that you should hit me.

Every day, **you tell me that you wish I was gone.** One day I'm going to go away and you're going to regret what you've done.

I love you with all my heart and I hate when we are apart. **It really hurts when I hear you don't love me.** I pour down tears when I'm in my room late at night. I wish you could comfort me and tell me how much you hate the way we fight.

I will love you **no matter what happens** with each other, because we will be together forever.

Roxanne, 14

A little girl has so much misery in her young life. She shouldn't have had **so much pain and neglect at her age.** Her parents have been traumatizing her and hitting her since the age of three. They aren't able to understand any choice their daughter makes or any words she chooses. **She feels alone.** She's in a world where her every thought is unheard by the people who should love her the most.

She feels like she is her own little family and the only one in her life. The pain is there on the inside and at home but if you see her, you'd think she is strong. On the street, her life would seem easy to live. Every day, after smiling with her friends, struggling at times to keep the tears in, she has to go home and deal with her parents. It's then she lets the tears out. **A light is shining in her life**, but where it's needed, there is dark, for her parents are the night.

Patricia

Daniel A., 15

It started off with screaming and yelling. My mom and dad argued about money and drugs. My mom had never been a druggie before she met my dad, who got her hooked on drugs. **My dad used to beat my mother every day.**

My sister was basically my mother from the time I was a year old. She raised me until I was about six.

The reason I was aggressive was because of the way my father treated my mother. But I couldn't be aggressive with him, so I was aggressive with others.

I led an aggressive life up to the age of fifteen. But for the past eight months, **I've been a different person.** I have been kind, caring and respectful to others in a way I never was before. I thank Leave Out ViolencE for that.

I wouldn't be here right now if I hadn't realized that I'm not alone, that there are other people out there in the same situation.

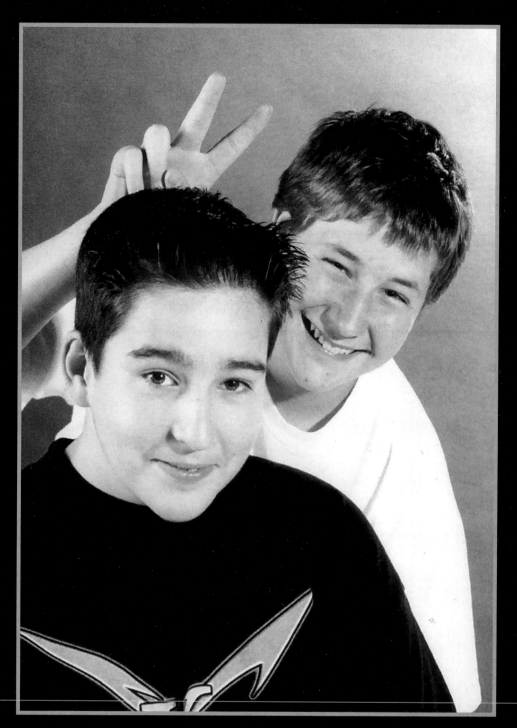

Chapter 5
School

Schools can be filled with tension and conflict; they can also be a refuge in a dangerous world. This chapter describes how schools can prevent — or encourage — a culture of violence.

Here are a number of voices from a round-table discussion on school:

School is a battleground. Everybody's cranky. The teachers. The students. There are all sorts of students who want to oppose you. **They judge you for who you are, for your skin color,** and they just want to take you down for who you are.

```
I feel safe
because I fight.
```

TEACHERS SHOULD TRY talking to kids, showing that they care and can be trusted. Then maybe the kid will open up and the teacher will be able to really help.

The only gang in our school are the bikers, because there are guys in our school who work for them. These kids come to school with their leather jackets. The teachers will tell them, "you're in school; take off that jacket." **But the teachers are afraid of the kids and so the kids** keep the jacket on anyhow.

Not every school is like that. **Half of my school is just peace & love.** If you don't want to get into a fight, you don't. It's all about image. If there is a fight, it's really about image; it's about little kids in grade seven or eight.

Sometimes, **fights start because the school is divided by national groups or races.** Somebody will go "oh the Greeks are stupid" or the Italians or whatever and that will start a fight... Or it can start during class with name-calling and back-stabbing and stuff like that.

Kimberly

I carry a knife. Not every day, but when I feel threatened. Like when there are a few kids out to get me.

You always have to worry because everybody judges you on how you look. When the new styles hit the popular people, everybody tries to copy them. But when the bottom group of people start wearing it, it all changes. They stay outcasts.

At our school it's not always just groups**, it's big gangs, fifty people** at a time. They paint graffiti everywhere and beat other people up.

At my school at recess kids will bother you for no reason. They bothered one kid who was part of a big gang. He told his friends, "let's go beat them up." That happens all the time.

I need respect and I'm not going to give it if I don't get it. **I hated teachers until I met a great teacher.** Felix. He helped me when I needed help. I even missed him during the summer. So I don't want to put up with all that saying that all authority figures are bad.

If I were a teacher, I would say, "You know something? If you can't appreciate the respect I'm giving you and I'm getting all this crap from you — good-bye. I hope you have a good life and don't end up in the gutter."

There's this teacher who is bright and sweet and joyful. She says that school is for us and not for her. **She takes her time;** she doesn't nag at you. Everyone gives her respect. **She cares.**

Anonymous, 17

Many students fear the crisp, cool wind that foretells the beginning of school. I was one of them. But for me, this year, **the fresher air and changing leaves tell me that there is a new chance,** a new beginning to a new life, and a hopeful future. I have overcome an awful past and will start off in a better place.

Not too long ago, I perceived the world as a place of hatred, darkness and sadness. **My perspective on the world was a bitter one.**

Previously a good Honour student, **I had turned into a drop-out.** No matter how many people told me how much potential I had, I shook it off and walked away. I thought I was being constrained, tied down to homework and exams. I was wrong. My days as a drop-out quickly began to seem more limiting than my previous days in school. I was always outside, **just hanging out and smoking endless packs of cigarettes.** My ritual every day was to crouch outside a pool hall, smoking and glaring at others as **they looked down on me** and my friends as if we were some kind of freaks.

DIFFERENT PEOPLE have different problems. No one should be condemned for looking for help, for trying to resolve his or her troubles.

We would sit outside in the cold or in a smoke-filled coffee shop, moaning and groaning about **how pitiful our lives were.** I was too caught up in my social circus to realize that the fun I was having would take two years out of my future. When **I made fun of my old friends for going to school**, I didn't realize that I was the real sucker. I'd ended my education for a day of meaningless fun with so-called friends.

I realize now **how horrible and meaningless those days were to me.** I would sit and freeze or I'd be in some confrontation with a person. I still can't believe that **I thought my old friends were jealous of me** because I was going out every day "having fun." Now I realize that I was the one who was jealous; I was jealous of all the potential, hopes and dreams that I once had and threw away.

The beautiful scenery of the autumn days reminds me of **laughter in the school yard and endless pages of homework.** Even though most people dread the thoughts and sounds of the beginning of a new school year, I am happy just knowing that I will be able to feel the smooth textbook covers, hear the sounds of a new book opening, and smell the freshly photocopied sheets of paper. **This is my chance** to prove to everyone that no matter how bad it got, **I am willing to fight back** for what I once had and what I will achieve.

This is a chance for me to have a happier and brighter future instead of just bumming around the dirty streets **doing absolutely nothing.** I want to leave behind **the bitterness, anger and despair that ran my life** for the past year. This I know I will achieve, because I am going to a better and happier place, a place of knowledge, laughter and a future — school. **I am strong and I will prevail** to be the girl I once was.

Anonymous

Tomzine, 17

If I was a teacher and I had a student in my class whose assignments were not being done, **who was arriving late for class,** and who, when he or she did show up, was unprepared — instead of an automatic detention, **I would try talking to the kid,** showing that I care and that **I can be trusted.** Then maybe the kid will open up to me and I can help.

Katie, 12

The problem with my school is that **some teachers always put us down.** One teacher told us that his ten-year-old son was better in math than our class. But it was the teacher's fault that **the majority of the class failed.**

Anonymous, 14

I feel that if I had nicer teachers I would do better in school. **I have one good teacher.** He's funny. Sometimes he yells at me for talking to my friends. But **he passes me because I do good work,** and sometimes he tells me that I do good work.

Sometimes it's the adults as much as the kids who encourage violent behaviour in school. At times, even school administration can be complicit.

Geoffrey, 15

This wasn't the first time Paul, my so-called friend, had done it: he and his friend would follow me to my bike and hold on to the back of it while **I tried to ride away.** When they would finally let me go, Paul would point at me from the sidewalk and laugh at me while the **two of them called me every name under the sun.**

Today, I decided to speak their language, to get back at Paul, the coward, **shove him up against the wall** and make him understand I didn't want any more bull-shitting around.

He thought he was safe because **he was standing beside the principal** when I ran towards him. Imagine his surprise when, instead of retreating, I just took him and **shoved him against the wall.**

Earlier, I had told the principal what was happening, and that this was what I might do. **She had agreed with me** that I should fight back, give him a good shove or something like that. **She actually said I should do it.** So I did. I was following the principal's advice when I slammed Paul up against the wall. The principal was two feet away all the time, watching.

IF THERE IS A FIGHT, it's really about image. If you don't want to get into a fight, you don't. It's all about image.

"Are you following me, you bastard?" I asked him.

"Yeah," he said calmly, though he wasn't calm. He was pissed off, surprised, worried, whatever…

He tried to get away but **I shoved him some more.** He stopped struggling and I shoved him along the wall into a bunch of framed school pictures. "Which side are you going out on?" I yelled at him.

"The front," he said calmly, even though **he was blushing more than before.** He then added, "I'll punch you."

"Really?" I once again yelled at him, and **grabbed his coat collar even tighter,** pushing him up against the wall on the opposite side of the corridor. I asked him angrily again, "Which way are you going out?"

"The back."

I was about to **punch him in the stomach** when I heard the principal say from behind me, "Stop! Now both of you go on; go home and eat lunch".

Still holding his collar, I asked him once again which way he was going out.

"The back."

He'd better. I turned around and **he turned around at the same time,** possibly to follow me out the front, but the principal pointed in the other direction.

"No, you go out that way," she said, "he's through with you." The guy turned around and went the other way. **Lucky that the principal had said this** or else I think I would have completely lost it.

Why did I do that? Well, after the whole affair, I walked home and thought about what had happened. I was following the principal's advice; **she was the one who'd agreed** that I should fight back.

Marie

Yellow Slips

Morgan, 18

My high school's student services department uses **yellow slips for its appointments.** For some students, these yellow slips are seen as being just another ordinary part of life. They believe that if a friend receives a yellow slip from the drug and alcohol counselor, the social worker or the family counselor, it simply means that the friend needs to talk to someone.

On the other hand, there are **other students who stereotype students who receive yellow slips** as being "troubled" or "different." Why would anyone take that attitude? Many adolescents have extremely difficult issues to deal with, and if having someone listen to your problems helps you, why should you be judged for that?

I NEED RESPECT from my teachers, and I'm not going to give it if I don't get it.

We should realize **how much courage it takes** to make an appointment on your own. Someone might not feel at all comfortable speaking with the school's guidance counselor, but **things have gotten so horrendous at home** that it's the only option. When this person receives a yellow slip in homeroom, people should not make them feel alienated. They shouldn't mistreat and stereotype a classmate because of a yellow slip.

Different people have different problems. No one should be condemned for trying to resolve his or her troubles. Period.

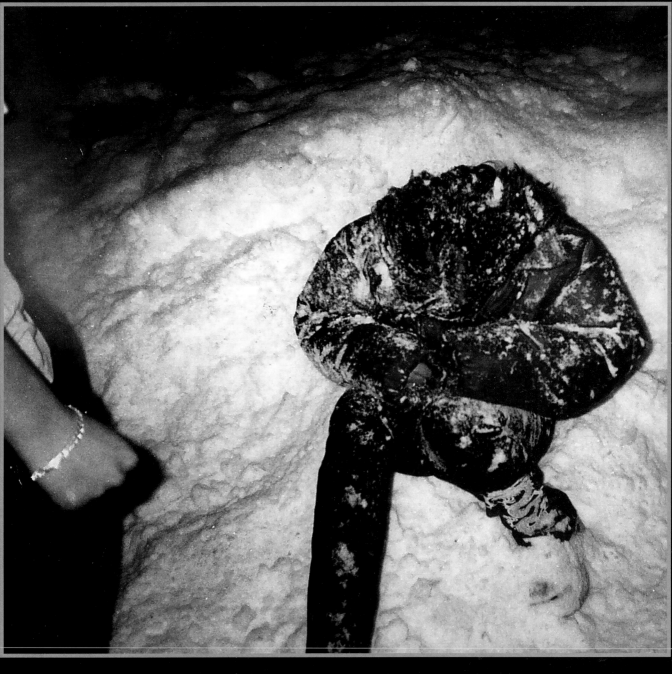

Chapter 6
Bullying

The bully and the bullied both speak out here. A former bully helps us understand why he acted as he did and how he turned his life around. The bullied speak of their pain and rage.

How Not to be a Target

Ali, 15

I never knew why **I was the target** in the playground. I thought it was the way I looked or where I came from. The first day of school I got punked off and **I said nothing**. That's when they knew: I was the new target. **I should have talked back and stood up for myself** but I didn't. Lunch time and gym were the worst times. I would get beat in the change rooms or deep in the fields where **the teachers were too scared to go.** My self-esteem went down like a big-ass rock falling from the CN Tower. Ninety-nine per cent of my life **I was discriminated against**, punked off and beaten. This bull-shit had to stop. **When I stood up for myself, it stopped.** It still happens sometimes, but you know what? — the hell with them. Yo — whoever is going through the same stuff: **drop your old friends who pushed you around** and find new ones. **Stand up for yourself,** be a somebody; don't let them push you around. That's my advice; take it and **you'll pull through,** trust me.

NOW, I GET ANGRY but I let it out in small ways, whether it be yelling or punching a wall. There's still violence, but it's not hurting someone. I don't go beating on people.

Daniel B., 18

Was I ever bullied? Hell, yeah. **I spent my entire grade five running**. Running to school, running from school, running from class to class, running from him. Not just any "him," it was Him. Him, **the only person able to strike fear in my heart,** the only person who could effectively remove my lunch money and outer clothing in less than ten words. It only took two: "Give me!" **His favourite hobby must have been robbing me,** because he did it often — and he was good at it, just like **I was good at running.** But sometimes I was just not fast enough. And that's when he got to practise his hobby and I lost my lunch money.

Marie-Claire

Vicki, 14

I used to bully a lot because it was the only way that I could show that I was a person too.

Alex A., 14

People forgive because there's **no point in holding a grudge.** The people who don't forgive don't understand that people make mistakes and we learn from mistakes. So don't take it personally if someone offends you. **Forgive and forget** and explain what went wrong so **it won't happen again.**

VIOLENCE IS NOT AN ANSWER. As much as you may think it is, it really isn't. You can lie to yourself for years but the fact of the matter is, it just is not it.

It Hurts More than Being Beaten Up

Amber, 16

I have been called names since before kindergarten and **it still goes on.** I think it hurts more than getting beat up. If I had the choice between someone calling me a name or kicking my ass, **I would choose to get my ass kicked.** It might sound crazy, but **I would rather have a scar on my face than on my heart.**

> FORGIVE AND FORGET and explain what went wrong so it won't happen again.

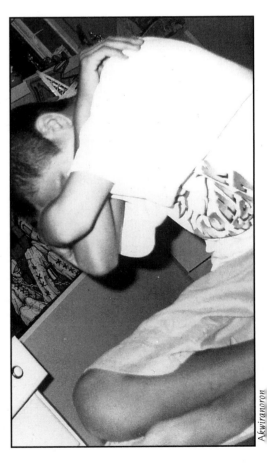

People call me ugly, fat, say I have big ears, that I'm short, self-centered. **I don't know what I'm doing wrong.**

People tell me all this stuff and **I act like I don't care,** but they don't know that **every time someone calls me a name, my heart breaks.** I tape the broken parts back together, but sooner or later there will be no more room left for tape.

I want people to see me for me. **I am a very scared child** and I just need a person to make me feel like me. **I need to feel like an equal**. I need my heart to heal.

Andrew's Story

Andrew tells us what drove him to bullying when he was younger, and how he came to realize that beating up on others didn't stop the pain he was feeling inside. Andrew, now 16, is a strong leader in the Leave Out ViolencE movement.

Because my dad was strict, **I always felt like he didn't love me;** I felt left out. If I think back now, I realize that he wasn't all that strict, but I was young then, and I didn't understand.

So, **I turned inward into my own little world** and tried to take out my anger towards my dad on other people.

On top of that, **I was picked on every day**, every day. I was picked on when I was a little kid in kindergarten. I can remember I was kicked, stood on, all because I kept to myself a lot. At first I developed more of **an inner anger that stayed contained inside of me.** It was like a depression or isolation. I didn't bother anyone else. **But I kept being pushed around, thrown around.**

Peggy

I always thought that it didn't really affect me but one day, **I just snapped.** That's when I became violent. It started when I got to grade one and two. One day this kid came up to me and said something like "f—k you," and **I just blew up.** I ran after him and beat him up. It was so unlike me and at the same time it *was* like me, because I was just so fed up. **I was so tired and frustrated that I lashed out.** From all the anger towards my dad, all the anger of being picked on and everything that had happened, I became a beast. **A floodgate opened up.**

Becoming violent didn't stop people from picking on me, but it kept them quiet. I had what I call "fake friends" who were friends only because they were scared of me. They still made comments behind my back and I still tended to beat them up, but not as severely.

Everything escalated in grade four when I moved in with my mother. There was this whole shift in parenting. I was let loose. With my dad, I had to be home at a certain time every day, but with my mom **I had more freedom.** So after school, I could go home, drop my bags, **pick up a baseball bat and go pick a fight;** whatever I wanted to do.

When I went to a new school, it all began to happen again. I was picked on and I turned inwards again. It was the same cycle exactly. I was different from the other kids there because they all had money;

ONE THING I SAY IS that you are not alone. You are never alone.

I did not. In the winter, I would wear shorts because I was warm enough and I would get picked on for that. I was big and I would get picked on for that. **I even got picked on because I was strong.** It was racism too at times. At that school at that time, all the kids were either French/Italian or pure French. I spoke Spanish and so I was left out. If I said something in Spanish, they would laugh at me.

At that time, **I still did not realize why I did the violence.** Now I do. I always thought it was because it was fun, because I liked it. **I didn't understand.** My excuse was that I liked the pure fight. It's hard to describe; it's like the pure adrenaline. It seems sick, twisted sometimes, but you know, I think it was the whole thing: the fight, **the sound of breaking bones.** It was exciting.

It was nothing that I'd learned in my home. A lot of people think that because I fight it is related to my parents but **it has nothing to do with my parents.** They never raised a hand towards me. So **you can't always blame families.** So if you are a bully, why are you a bully? Well, **I am a bully because I am angry at the world,** because other people hit me, because…it's many things. I felt that my dad was too strict on me and maybe my dad missed out on the stuff I did.

During the summer, I would go downtown, and if anyone even looked at me funny, **I would blow up on them.** I would hurt them big time, close to near

Zico

death; just beating the crap out of some-body with my bare hands. I believed if you're going to fight, fight with bare hands, not weapons. But **if someone brought a weapon, I'd bring a weapon too.** But never a gun or a knife; I would never go to those extremes. There was always something holding me back, saying **"don't kill some-body."** I gave them broken bones, broken jaws, broken noses, swollen eyes, broken ribs, punctured things.

Even if I beat somebody bad, though, I still had the heart to call an ambulance. But I would never go and visit them in the hospital afterwards. **There were no criteria for my victims.** If you were tall, I didn't like you, I picked on you. If you looked funny, I picked on you. You had more money than me, I picked on you. You had something I wanted, I picked on you. You got something I wanted, I stole it from you. **It didn't matter; it really didn't matter.** There were no criteria. I didn't just pick on someone because they were vulnerable; it just didn't matter.

Younger kids didn't want to stay around me. **I felt feared.** I knew they feared me and I liked it. I started my own gang, the standard bully-with-his-friends kind of thing. My own little crew. Leaders are the tough ones. When I talked I demanded authority. **I despised authority and yet when I talked I demanded it.** It was just my manner and my tone of voice and the way I stood. I would do the intimidating. In high school, I would just pick on people at random. Once, this kid made fun of me and all of a sudden — boom — I chased him down, and boom, boom. I just went click.

My mother didn't know. I was never home. I would come and go as I pleased. I always knew how to mask myself from my mom. Sometimes, it would leak through a little, **but not enough to make her worried.** She never really knew what was going on. I knew how to hide my injuries and most of the time they were not facial blows, but more like body shots.

At that time, **I also broke windows, did fires, pushed kids off a hill, broke arms.** From stealing at stores, to cars, to breaking into houses, I have never been caught for anything.

I had that attitude because **I was confused**. I didn't really know what I wanted. I didn't really know who I was. Basically, I was moving — switching cities, switching parents — **we constantly moved and so many things just built up in me.** I was just confused. I was lost in my own world. I didn't feel a sense of anything because I was bouncing around from my mom to my dad. I never really felt at home, like, "this is where I live; this is where I will grow up." I was bounced from place to place. I never really felt a sense of connection to a special place.

> STAND UP FOR YOURSELF, be a somebody; don't let them push you around. When I stood up for myself, the bullying stopped.

I am not confused any more, though. If anything, I feel more of a connection to myself and **I don't get involved like I used to between my mother and my father when they have spats.** I found that emotionally draining. I used to keep it inside until I would blow up. **Now, I get angry but I let it out in small ways,** whether it be yelling or punching a wall. There's still violence, but it's not hurting someone. I don't go beating on people. **I don't end up putting people in the hospital.** I am not hurting anybody. I can now see the actual pain of hurting someone and I can see it in myself too.

Not only was I the bully and someone else the victim, but I was the victim myself. I may have beaten someone else up because they insulted me, but I always had low self-esteem, so that when I would beat up on someone, I was not mad at them, I was mad at myself, I was mad at life. Every time I beat up on someone, it was,

"now you know how I feel; take some of my pain." But it never really worked out like that. It was not really taking out my pain. It was just beating the shit out of someone. Not the most pleasant of experiences for them.

As a member of L.O.V.E., **I have begun to open up a lot more.** I opened up to some young kids; I feel great knowing that **I've actually touched other kids.** They can relate to what I've been through, because **they're going through the same thing.**

One thing I say is that **you are not alone.** You are never alone. No matter how much you may think you are, there's always at least a good ten other people in the world going through the exact same thing you are. When you're in the state of mind I was in at the time, **you feel isolation and depression,** and to know you're not alone is a big thing. To know that **someone else is going through the same thing** you are, that someone else understands you, is something that would have been big for me. **Violence is not an answer.** As much as you may think it is, it really isn't. You can lie to yourself for years but the fact of the matter is, it just is not it.

Even when you get away with it, **it ends up hurting you more than anyone else.**

Patricia

Chapter 7
Drugs

When young people's lives are filled with anger and grief, escape into drugs has its appeal. But the stories in this chapter show how drug use only tightens the vicious cycle of abuse, violence and despair; they also point to a way out of the cycle.

Photo on previous page by Jonathan

It's a Tough Road Back

It's a Tough Road Back
Back

Tiffany B., 15

Hard drugs have been a large part of my life ever **since I was twelve.**

When I was thirteen, I walked in on **my brother** while he **was smoking heroin.** I broke down and started crying. Finding out that he was smoking heroin and drinking every day was hard on me.

On my fifteenth birthday I got home drunk and went to sleep. When I woke up, **I found out my sister was dead.** That night I went out and drank again; my mom was drinking too. For around **eight days straight, I drank with my friends** and three of my cousins. My mom drank at home with my step-dad and older cousin.

My mom and I found out a few days ago that **my brother had lied to the police** when he said that my sister had died of a cocaine overdose. **It was really heroin,** and he gave it to her. After I found that out I had to leave my house. Again, I drank.

I drink because it **helps me forget how much I'm hurting** inside. I know even as I drink that the pain will be there when I wake up, but **I just drink again**. I don't think I can forgive my brother for killing our sister.

MUSIC HEALS the body, mind and soul. Music sets your spirit free.

After my sister's death, alcohol was a very big part of my life. I stopped listening to my mom and stopped respecting what she said.

I've tried to tone down my drinking. **It was hard going from drinking every day to drinking once in a while,** but I've done it. Now I'm working on going to school and listening to my mom.

This will be a tough climb, but **I'm sure I can make.** I know I can make it.

Kim

Kym, 17

Madness arises as I get out of bed. **People frustrate me,** and a lot of the time I hate them for no reason. Why? **Parents destroying my life,** brother leaving me behind like I was a hungry man asking for loose change. I don't need anyone, I say. I have to stop lying to myself. **I need someone, anyone.** Punch the door, scream and yell, cry. Escape reality, have a beer or two or three or more.

Suzy, 19

I believe that music heals the body, mind and soul. No matter what mood you are in or what you are feeling, the music will take you and help you get through it. **Drugs and alcohol take life away.** Music sets your spirit free.

INSTEAD OF DESTROYING my brain and spinal cord and nervous system, I'd rather spend a night with someone on the beach or wherever we could be, alone, just chilling and talking.

Anonymous, 16

It was a gloomy Saturday night; my friends and I had gone to a party. The place was packed; over seventy people crammed into two hotel rooms. **It was crazy.** Pizza on the floor, empty liquor bottles on the bed, Zig-Zag packages strewn around: it was a disaster.

I saw some people I hadn't seen in years, but they weren't really themselves, because they were either drunk or high. My friends and I were getting ready to go because the party was starting to get lame. As we were leaving, we heard some arguing but we just ignored it.

We were saying our good-byes when **we heard a scream coming from downstairs**. A crowd rushed to the window to see what was going on. I could see **someone on the ground** with a herd of people around him. My friends and I ran down to see what had happened.

As the elevator door opened, we heard someone say, "Call 911." I saw my friend's hat on the cold bare cement. **My heart dropped**. I ran as fast as I could to where he was lying motionless on the ground. It was the most horrifying moment of my life. One of my friends was on the ground and **I couldn't tell if he was breathing or not.**

I fell to my knees and screamed, "It's not fair, it's not fair." My friend was an excellent guy. How could someone do this to him? He didn't deserve this.

The paramedics showed up soon after. When they got there, they found out that he was still breathing. He was taken to hospital breathing but still not conscious. I was scared to death for him.

My friend had a **total of seven stab wounds,** seventy-nine stitches and a month of therapy. He's fine now and still the same guy I knew before this all happened. But they **still don't know who or why or how this happened.**

It was hard going from drinking every day to drinking once in a while, but I've done it. Now I'm working on going to school and listening to my mom. This will be a tough climb, but I'm sure I can make. I know I can make it.

MY SUBSTITUTE FOR LOVE

Mohammed, 19

Sink into my blood

Come on

Make me feel good

Make me feel loved

Make me feel safe

Care about me

Touch me with your warm hand

Tease me

Make me feel appreciated

Stand behind me when I fall

Tell me you love me

Sophie

Mohammed's Story

Mohammed, 19

Who ever thought life was going to be this hard? **Not just hard, but difficult as hell.** I sometimes think no one in this world will ever understand me. No one will ever be able to understand another person completely, because **we all have such different experiences.** Who am I going to find to understand me, if I even want that? What I do want, however, is someone I can spill my guts out to. **Someone I can tell my deepest fears, thoughts or feelings.** Someone to love or fall in love with. I'm in love with drugs, but that sucks. It's not real love. **I want to care about someone,** but that opportunity has not been given to me yet.

Failure in many ways; failure in all ways. **I hate failing at everything** I do. I failed life. Failed myself at helping myself. I never got anywhere. Failed at school. The future — I don't know. **I don't want to fail any more.** But once a failure always a failure. And if it continues this way then I want to die, be killed, anything that'll put an end to this **constant intense pain of failure.**

I'M LEARNING TO DEAL with the hand I've been dealt. Reality is where I belong; I'm learning to cope, and realizing that things can't go right all the time.

You're what keeps me going every day. You're what puts a smile on my face. You're what makes life worth living. You're what makes me forget the evil. **You're what I think about every hour of every day.** Even in my dreams you sometimes appear; you're what makes my heart pound. You're what makes me jump with joy. You give me warmth. You make me feel wanted. **You're only made of chemicals.** I wish you had a face and body. But I still love you with all my heart.

I'm so sick of it. **I am so sick of having to get high to enjoy life.** It's so sad. I'm going to waste with this drug habit. I can't even stand up straight any more. This artificial high is pathetic. I pop a pill and enjoy the next three hours of life **only to get depressed and feel like I want to die later on.** Coming back to reality is the worst, realizing that your situation is not as happy and good as it seems when you're insanely high on drugs. And **you don't even know what's in those drugs.** I've done the harshest and dirtiest of drugs. I know that in a few days, I'll be craving more.

I did hard drugs on the weekend, **really dirty drugs.** I'm about to collapse onto the ground. I've got a headache. **I've got no power at all.** I can't walk straight. My stomach is about to explode. **I can't think.** The headache is from all the dead brain cells. Drugs f—k you up like they are doing it to me right now. I've got a bad backache and neck ache. **Who knows how bad my brain is affected.**

DON'T DO DRUGS!

I never thought I'd get this far into drugs. It started with a little joint and moved on to **some of the most dangerous drugs in the world,** like crystal meth and a bunch of others. It's **the lack of a loving environment** that made me go this way and also a lack of fear and a curiosity about the different highs. My life came down to either love from people or drugs. **I didn't feel love from people.** No one was there to show it to me or even ask me what I was feeling. I lost Rob. Big loss. Then I f—ked up and did ecstasy to replace Rob. All I want is Rob back in my life or a replacement. Till then I don't know what I'll do: **try to stay away from harsh drugs,** but how?

Instead of going to a rave and **destroying my brain and spinal cord and nervous system,** I'd rather spend a night with someone on the beach or wherever we could be, alone, just chilling and talking.

But that's a dream.

I'd like to be high on life, not high on drugs all my life. **I want to have sober fun.**

Anonymous, 16

My childhood? I don't know about my childhood. **I had an alcoholic father who was very abusive.** He was very, very abusive. He would go on big drinking binges and I would see him maybe once a week when he was sober. When he came home drunk, he would be very **verbally and physically abusive with my mother.** I just sort of saw it all. Towards me it was more verbal abuse. Very controlling type of guy.

My mother was always pretty cool, but she had to deal with all that and **she had cancer when I was little, maybe four.** The cancer went into remission when I was about seven or eight. So I was just basically there. I don't know how it made me feel. I was a little kid so I never thought anything of it; I thought it was normal. **As a kid I never used to play.** I would read, do whatever. **My sister helped me through a lot of it**; she was my mentor. And then, I don't know, maybe she couldn't take it. She's been on the streets since she was about twelve. She's twenty-one now. She does a lot of drugs; **she's into heroin.** She used to be a prostitute. She's got HIV now; she has a child. She's pregnant. **She still influences my life a lot.**

I started **smoking a lot of weed when I was ten.** The first time I got high, it was just so carefree; it felt really good. I got the weed from my sister. We went and smoked a joint at school. Everyone was, like, "you're so cool." I think it's a power trip for little kids, because you're, like, — **wow, you're so cool**. And then it wasn't weed alone; I was an alcoholic. **I was about twelve, thirteen.** I had my first drink when I was around eleven. We stole it from my best friend's grandparents' house. It tasted really bad. We took a little bit from every bottle so they wouldn't notice and filled up a two-litre. We went out with my friend's older brother and partied with him. And **that night I fell down the stairs.** It was really weird.

I'd like to be high on life, not high on drugs all my life. I want to have sober fun.

Then I would have drinking binges that would go on for days, two, three weeks — different party every night. My drinking binges, when I look back, they were sort of fun. When I started they were fun. Just people getting together, throwing parties at houses. It was a kind of freedom, I guess. The state of mind that you're in, you don't care; you don't care about anything. You just have fun; you don't think about whatever is going on. What I thought about when I wasn't drunk was that I wanted to be drunk. Sometimes, coming off it was so harsh on your body; I would just lie there. It was almost as if I had this hurting in me, my body was hurting, and it was so hard to think, and all you need is that one drink and your body won't feel all crazy. After a while, it wasn't as fun as it had been.

I didn't go to school. I started dropping out a lot around grade seven; six or seven. And then I slowly started doing lines. I was fourteen. I started hanging out with these Spanish guys, partying with them, going on binges. If I was drunk, I would do a lot of things, because

you don't really think about it. The first time I did a line, I was pretty drunk. I didn't like it, the feeling; my head was pounding. I didn't really like the feeling. I didn't do it again for a while, but then, it's like — everyone else is doing it. It seemed like a sort of invisible pressure. I've done a lot of coke, I've smoked point seven, which is like heroin. Point seven is really easy to get. Pretty addictive too, because you start it and it seems like the ultimate high. It's not a downer. A lot of people who do it for the first time just don't like it because it's a terrible feeling.

But **once you start doing it, you eventually want something cheaper,** so you go for D. D is heroin. It's a down; you can smoke it, shoot it, whatever.

It was the worst time. **There were good days, there were bad days,** especially for my boyfriend, who supplied me. I met him through my sister. I thought I loved him, but it was more like control. **Because he had the drugs, he controlled me.** It was a really bad sort of relationship. He used to sell. We would go on his route into the States, and we would trade cocaine for weed. Me, I wouldn't really have to do anything. I would just be in the van, and we would just go, and I would get a few bucks. **We were pretty stupid at times,** because we would just have it in the back seat or underneath the car in empty car parts. **I was a juvenile,** and the authorities couldn't really touch me; that's probably why they brought me in. Cops will put their punches in on people who are older, but they couldn't really touch me.

I've seen a lot of violence. Basically, there were a lot of B & E's — break and enters. Sometimes they would take three minutes. I'd just be in the car. My boyfriend would stop the car, he'd see a house, and — boom — he'd go in and come out with TVs, VCRs, and then we'd just drive along like **it was a normal part of life.** If he was high or something he would have a temper. Or if things weren't right or on command or the way he wanted, then **he would start screaming, punch walls.** He never really hit me that much, but still, he was verbally abusive. He didn't really hit me that much. If he was really pissed or drunk or high or something he might. Or this once — I don't know what the heck I was doing, but I dropped a box, a Tupperware, and the bottom cracked. And **he blew up.** You know, no one should be hit, but he wasn't hitting me every day. That's probably why I stayed with him. **I would think, well, it doesn't happen that often.** I was with him for almost a year.

I just up and left one day. I was seeing this guy and this girl. **I was really close to her.** We used to do normal things together; **I could be a kid with her.** We would do laundry or a movie. Even though we'd slip all these mickeys in, we'd go and watch movies and just talk. **One day she disappeared.** I'm pretty sure someone got her. You know, it was just .... people around me were dying and I could see my sister going deeper and deeper and I thought you know, **I don't want to be like that.** One day I just saw that that was how I was going to be.

Like I said, **my sister got into prostitution.** She got HIV, which scared the shit out of me. **That scared me so bad when she got HIV.** It really shocked me. It's not like I freaked out or anything, but it was just another thing to add to her problems. I think after that, she got more into drugs because **she didn't really care.** She figured, "I'm going to die anyway, so who really cares?" She can blow $900 in two days. She'll go into recovery sometimes, especially when she runs out of money. She'll be **in and out of recovery,** but it never lasts. I don't know what to feel when I see her; it hurts… Every time I see her it hurts.

I first started to get out of drugs because for the first time in my life, I was deprived of them. **I found myself not having the money to buy.** For two months, three months, I was just on the street, living on the street. I don't know why I didn't go to live at home. **I sort of felt ashamed,** like, why go home? That and I realized when I was home I was never happy anyway. I would be with different guys, different friends, in

Christine

these little crappy apartments and I would stay there with different people. I stayed a lot with this one girl who took me in. **She could be really mean;** she could be pretty mean. I stayed a lot with her even though I realized I couldn't live in a ten by ten room for the rest of my life.

In terms of getting out, **I was basically a self-help case.** It took a lot of will power. **It was a decision that I made at a certain point.** I still don't really know how I did it. It was **seeing all these people dying.** I was the one per cent of the people down there to get out of it. I knew I could because I realized that **my life to begin with wasn't that bad.** I realized that I shouldn't be putting myself through this and I didn't want to get any diseases. I did it because **I was not really a heavy user.** I think that's why I was able to get out. I would go through one to four lines a day. Then for a long time there I did a line or two a day.

Just getting down to that, I was the ultimate bitch. It hurt; my body hurt. This aching, throbbing pain throughout your whole body. And I had really bad cold sweats and jitters and twitching arms. I couldn't eat, I couldn't handle any food — not Jell-o; nothing. I went to a clinic downtown where they help you through that, and I was put into a recovery house for six weeks.

Now, I really struggle with going to school. I go to an alternative school. It's all right. I've been writing a lot. People say I'm a good writer. Seriously, I might get into being a lawyer. I really want to change the way people think, so people will see what really goes on. A lot of people walk by someone and say, "she's just another junkie on the street." They have no idea of what actually goes on, why people are there. People don't know; they don't know about circumstances. People say, "why don't they just get a job?" You know, it's not that easy; you can't just quit your addiction and go get a job and live what society portrays as a normal life.

Myself, I would love to go down there and get everyone off the street, because no one deserves to live that way, so terrible.

Patricia

Sheena, 16

I used to be a daily user of drugs. **You name it: I've done it.** Anything I could get my hands on that would get me high I'd use; anything from marijuana to heroin. Now I regret it, because it **has killed thousands of brain cells.** I used to steal from my friends, my family and strangers. If it wasn't money, **I'd steal any item that was worth money.** I would do it just to get my fix.

When you're high, **you have no feelings;** you don't know what you're doing. You're lost in your own little world, trying to find a very peaking high. I used to live on the streets using drugs and alcohol. **You can get sick, even die.** I thank God for helping me get clean.

That's why I'm writing this story. The only reason I used narcotics and alcohol was **to take my mind away from my problems.** That's why I say the use of narcotics is a mind game, not an addiction. It's just crazy. **I've lost a bunch of close friends** just recently due to the use of heavy narcotics.

IN TERMS OF GETTING OUT, I was basically a self-help case. It took a lot of will power. It was a decision that I made at a certain point. It was seeing all these people dying.

Finally, I had the courage to change. **I had to hit rock bottom** before I could realize that I needed help. Unfortunately, I had to find help on my own, because I had lost so much trust in people. **I have now finally gained more trust back.** But the point of this story is to stop youth and kids from using harmful narcotics. It's not worth it, because you just close the doors and windows of opportunity.

I've left behind **a world where I'd only imagined that there were no problems,** it was all happiness. I'm learning to deal with the hand I've been dealt. **Reality is where I belong;** I'm learning to cope, and realizing that things can't go right all the time.

Chapter 8
Relationships

In this chapter, our writers describe the dangerous places that love has taken them and their struggles to break free. They write also about the joy that caring for someone can bring.

Photo on previous page by Maureen Rodriguez Labreche

Anonymous, 16

It was two days after we met that **you told me you loved me.** It took me three days to say the same to you, afraid that my words would destroy it all, but I finally did — the first time I had spoken it aloud to anyone, **the first time that I had ever wanted to.** I knew then that I had relinquished all control of myself to you. From then on, **everything I did would depend first on you.** People called to each other, someone shoved against me, and the fluorescent lights flickered far above my head as I voiced the words back to you. **I smelled of lavender** and as you pulled me into your arms, the thought flickered at the back of my head that **you could crush me** with a single action.

It was shortly after I admitted that I loved you that I discovered my ability to **find you in everything.** A streak of sun would glint on a thickness of red hair; someone would hurry by, their height hunched; the skin around someone's eyes would crumple like **dried roses crushed between my fingers.** My heart would flip, thinking it was you, knowing it wasn't, and then **the illusion would pass.** There would be a deep

Patricia

wrenching inside, and, if I wasn't already on my way to see you, I would hurry to a pay phone to call you. I would call you several times a day, and **you would always be there to answer.** It was as though you waited for me, lived for me.

When I spoke to you, my words sliding down the telephone lines, I would suffer through the images of **you with someone else, stroking another girl's hair** even as you whispered endearments to me. In public, I would hold on to you, wanting to announce to the world that, yes, **you were mine, no one else's,** and I was yours, and it would always be that way. I would sometimes imagine laughter as we walked by together, thinking everyone except me knew you were with someone else. Your true love. That during the night and whenever you weren't with me, **you would be with her.** I would picture you holding yourself over her, your fingers indenting her thighs, her hands sliding up and down your back; that when next I saw you, **your skin would be fresh from her touches,** and the smell of her perfume — sandalwood, lilac, orange-flavored — would swirl around my head.

I found out that what I thought was love was really obsession, and what I thought was protection was really control.

I would dial your number at three in the morning, reassured that **your voice was thick with sleep,** and that you were willing to emerge from the webs of dreams to sing me lullabies and repeat that you loved me until I was tired.

I have learned to stay away from you. **It has been six months** and when I am away from you, the numbness overcomes me and I am almost able to forget what we had and how much I want it back. **I sit apart at school** and try to discourage the tentative friendships that have formed around me. **Nights are scheduled:** slots for exercising, studying and grooming. Hours are filled until three or four in the morning, when I have finally worked myself into such exhaustion that I am not afraid to sleep.

It is when I talk to you that it is hard. **Everything rushes back,** waves of longing crashing over my soul. If your new love isn't around, you're both tender and caring. Worried about my going out into the cold of the winter, **you draw my hood over my hair,** ask if I'd like to borrow a scarf — looking into my eyes as you say this with the eyes that once asked so desperately if I loved you. You still sometimes say that I never loved you. **You move towards me and put your arms around me,** a physical good-bye which seems somehow longer and more careful than those I share with others. You hug me as **though I were made of glass.** It takes me at least a week to readjust, to return to my scheduled emotions.

When she is around you turn mean: **mocking comments and nasty jokes,** deliberate attempts to hurt me. Sometimes, you'll reach back in time and dredge up what we once had and use it against me, all the while looking at her for reassurance. It is as though you are proving to her that **you care nothing for me,** that your world would be so much better if I moved south and west to the other end of the continent, where I could never bother you. **It hurts.** I respond to the hurt, and tell someone, usually one of your former friends, what an awful person you are. They will agree, telling me stories about how **much you've changed** since being with her, how you enjoy putting others down, watching others flinch from your words. After it has been agreed that you're no longer good, **I put down the receiver** and pad to either the kitchen or the bathroom, where I will choose between cramming as much junk into my body as possible or slicing off as much flesh as possible. Whichever I choose, the other usually follows, unless I **pass out from exhaustion first.**

And each time, **I try to convince myself** that you are nothing to me.

I NEVER ASKED FOR A PUNCH in the face, a kick in the ribs or a push down the stairs. I was blind to the signs of the potential danger of my boyfriend's controlling behaviour, and I ended up full of fear.

Pat, 15

She was the one for me, or so I thought. I would have given her anything. I can't remember how many nights I spent thinking about her. I can't count how many times she cried on my shoulder, or **the hours we spent on the phone.** Then finally, I had my chance. I didn't know I'd be the one crying or that I was being played for a fool. I loved her with all my heart and I didn't see any of it. **I can't count how many times I've cried** or how many times I've wanted to kill myself. I thought maybe if I faked my own death and changed my personality, my looks, everything about me, then I would get another chance with her. Then I realized that if my girlfriend didn't like me for who I was, **she wasn't worth it.** So, maybe later on I'll find someone who does like me for who I am.

Pauline

Anonymous, 16

THE GUILT AND SHAME grew inside my body as I lay in the corner of what I considered my jail cell. I cried and rocked myself to sleep, praying to a God that I had never before believed in. I lost count of the days of repetition, **the endless days** of the bittersweet love/hate relationship that I was involved in.

At first it was like heaven. I was showered with compliments and gifts. We were both popular; we were "the" couple. Things started getting serious and he became the love of my life. So **I was flattered when he would beat up another guy** just for glancing at me.

But I found out that what I thought was love was really obsession, and what I thought was protection was really control.

The first time he assaulted me — because I had accepted an invitation to a party — **he pushed me down a flight of stairs**. I was knocked unconscious. After, he apologized endlessly. That same night I broke up with him and he smashed my face into a brick wall. His apologies came with tears; he described his actions as an accident. I explained the damage to friends as an accident I'd had while roller-blading drunk.

I was so blind and trusting that instead of giving up on my boyfriend, I gave up on myself, and I lost something that I can never get back.

I never asked for a punch in the face, a kick in the ribs or a push down the stairs.

I was blind to the signs of the potential danger of his controlling behaviour, and I ended up full of fear. Fear for my life, my family and my future.

Valerie, 16

I WAS IN LOVE WITH A MONSTER. **I was so blind and trusting** that instead of giving up on him, I gave up on myself, and I lost something that I can never get back.

With every **punch, scratch and degrading name,** I became a victim.

I was slowly becoming a statistic.

Sometimes I wonder **what would have happened** if the police hadn't arrested him that night.

What if he had killed me, or someone else? Sometimes, when I close my eyes, **I can feel his presence.** It sends chills through my body.

I remember **the fear and frustration that I felt.** I sense the power and control that he had over me. **I was afraid of his anger,** but in love with his heart. I believe that the hostility and anger that I developed towards the end of our relationship was what kept me going.

I'm so confused. **He's a part of my past that I can never forget.** I'm bitter and I have so much hate for that time in my life, the loss of my innocence. I try so hard every day to regain it. **I'm different; too different.** I wasn't given a choice. It's been a long time and I've begun to heal but sometimes, when I close my eyes, I get lost.

I REALIZED that if my girlfriend didn't like me for who I was, then she wasn't worth it.

THE BOYFRIEND

Laura, 15

Yet another one did it;
he just came out and said it.
What did I do? What made him do it?
I just want to know.
Was it because I said "no"?
That's all I want to know.
He won't call me, or even say hi to me.
So yet another did it, just came out and said it.
What did I do; what made him do it?

INDIFFERENCE

Gary, 19

What sad event of yesterday,
what terrible scar
keeps you from caring?
Was there a time when dreams
lived inside you?
Didn't hope once fill your heart?
I know that disappointment is painful,
and you want to protect yourself
from its cruel sting.
You think that if you don't care,
you can't get hurt.

Well, when you harden your heart,
you may not feel the pain,
but you're not feeling anything
else either. Is that the way you
want to live?

Invite people into your heart.
Let our love be the balm that
softens the scars and soothes
your wounds. Let compassion
fill you up and be a gift
that you share with others.
Know that you are valued and cared for.
Now you must value
and care for yourself.

Katie, 12

A friend is having someone around **TO LAUGH AND GIGGLE WITH**. Love is having a friend hugging you and TELLING YOU THAT IT IS ALL RIGHT WHEN YOU CRY.

Nathalie

So Unsure

Morgan, 18

one look in her dark eyes
and you see the spark, the fire
she's done a good job
at masking and suffocating it

I know better than to believe
that she's silently drifting away
because the storm hasn't hit yet...
her hurricane is nearing, nearing

She's my pansy girl
so beautiful yet so
    unsure...

yeah, she's the real deal
as vivid as dancing
swirling naked in the rain

she's here in my thoughts, my dreams
she knows that I'll never let go
what we have is stronger than any f—king hurricane

she's my pansy girl,
so beautiful yet so
    unsure...
          and I wonder what it's like to be her.

RECONCILIATION

Sheena, 16

It's about time we reconcile,
Bring our faces back to a smile.
One month seems like forever,
But now again we're back together
Erase all the mishaps from the past,
This time we're going to make
Our friendship last.

Zico

Chapter 9
Gangs

Joining a gang can seem like a way out of loneliness, a way to find family and home. In this chapter our writers, some of them former gang members, explore and expose the seduction; they also demonstrate how the violence and crime that gang culture fosters offers no genuine solutions in the end.

Revenge

A Heavy Lesson in Revenge

Alex B., 16

The aluminum baseball bat comes crashing down on the victim's head, splitting it open. Too much for any human to endure. As I am witnessing this horrible act being committed by my friends, I'm wondering to myself, **why am I not feeling bad for this person?** What human being am I?

As I go to sleep, I hear the phone ring. I pick it up: "Hello?" "You're f—king dead!" The guy hangs up. Who the hell was that? I go to sleep not knowing that the person who just called is a friend of the person who got hit over the head with the baseball bat.

All of a sudden I wake up to the sound of breaking glass. My windows have been smashed, my house violated. Too many thoughts race through my mind. Who would have the nerve to do this? Despite the **rage I feel inside,** despite wanting to kill the people who have just vandalized the home that my parents have worked so hard for, I realize that it was *us* **who brutally beat their friend,** who violated *them*.

I HAD TO GET OUT because it was killing me.

All this sickens me. I have participated in and have witnessed too much for my age and I can bear no more. Sometimes I just want to leave — not die, but just go somewhere far, far away from everything, so I can start my life over. But no matter where I go, I can never turn my back on the problem; it'll always be here.

Angela, 16

I knew a boy who went to my school. **He always treated me kindly**; never once was he rude or hateful. **He seemed very quiet and distant.** When he saw me in the hall, he would always stop me just to say hi. Until I read about him in the newspaper, I would have never known that **he had that secret in his life.** So smart, so creative. Talent and wisdom beyond his years. I guess there wasn't enough talent and wisdom in the world to keep him alive. **He was stabbed during a fight** in a night club. It was gang-related.

Pat, 15

I was in a gang, but **I'm not any more.** I had to get out because **it was killing me.** They wanted me to do stuff that I didn't want to do, like steal cars, break and enter, shoplift... They also wanted me **to try harder drugs.** I almost said yes. They asked me to smoke crack, do coke... The reason I didn't was because **I didn't want to end up in a hospital bed,** not knowing where I was because I overdosed on cocaine or crack.

Ferdousi, 17

Sometimes we are so consumed by **what is wrong with society** that we pull ourselves away, **not letting ourselves be a part of it,** and not realizing that we are becoming what is wrong with it.

Anonymous, 16

Violence robs your soul. **Violence threatens your life.** With violence, you always have to look behind you. You can beat violence with **love, friendship and peace.**

Peggy

Jeremy's Story

When Jeremy told this story to L.O.V.E., he was on probation for break and enter and possession of a weapon. He has decided that he wants an honest, simple life, but he still has to struggle every day to play it straight.

Just ask my mother —she knows that **I did break and enters at age five:** first my friend's house and then my neighbours'. I wasn't stealing anything, I was just in there to be nosy.

I think I was rebelling. **I needed to see my father,** who left when I was four or five. He just took off. I remember going to his hotel room on his second wedding and camping out in the front hallway, banging on the door, asking to be seen. He didn't want to see me. So I just rebelled against everything.

I was angry, and what I was aiming for was to get some sort of attention, some sort of positive attention, not the negative kind. That was what I was getting from my stepfather who'd come on the scene right at the same time. My mom had been going through a big argument with my dad, and the next thing I know, a couple of months later my mom takes off to be married and comes back with my step-dad who's a drunk, an alcoholic, and likes using the rubber hose…

We lived in a trailer house, a motor home. **We were rednecks,** but it was a pretty nice neighbourhood. There were maybe ten houses on our block and we were the only trailer house on the whole block. It was pretty decent. I just had to walk down from my backyard, and I'd be right in front of my school. **I had my own room;** my friends could come over whenever they wanted.

The issue was more with my stepfather. **I didn't like him; he didn't like me.** He didn't do much for a living. His father had a big farm and the whole family were pretty much alcoholics. **He'd go there all day and drink** and take care of the farm and then come home and drink some more.

My mom worked at a shoe company with my dad, but when they divorced, she couldn't look at his face any more, so she quit. She became a caterer, then a seamstress; whatever odd jobs she could manage to do around the house. I remember sitting with her watching "All My Children" when I didn't feel like going to school or I'd been kicked out or something .

You don't really know what you're getting into when you're being courted by the gang.

My mom is **one of those "my-way-or-the-highway" type of people.** And sometimes my plan is a little bit better and sometimes hers is, but we butt heads a lot because we're both about the same. Other than that, **she's a pretty nice person.** She's been through a lot.

She did what she had to do to take care of her kids. She wasn't a bad mom even though there were times when I thought so, because she was really getting into doing the beatings with my stepfather. It's one of those things you have to deal with when you're growing up.

My dad was a real racist.

I can't say anything else other than that. Yeah, he had ties to the Klan and ties to a couple of other things. **He's a straight-up racist.** He's not kind to other people and he didn't take care of his kids.

I remember the only thing that I did with him as son-father deal was going fishing when I was younger. But because I was making too much noise, smashing around the water, **he threw me in the car** and went back to fishing himself. And I spent the rest of the day in the car. I ignored that he'd thrown me in the car and focused on the fact that **I was with my dad,** having a good time. **I lived off that for a while.**

When I moved away, **everything changed.** I got new friends, I got to ... not prove myself, but to make myself new friends there. It was just different. I didn't have time to think about crime; **I didn't really care about crime at that time.** I was trying to make friends, get to know my neighbourhood, get to know the city.

I was hoping I could become something. Now that my family had moved out of the backwoods and were living in a city, **maybe we**

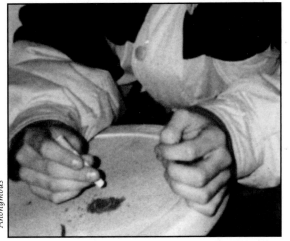

Anonymous

could make something of it, be people, normal people, instead of being the redneck family with the drunk alcoholic stepfather beating his kids. I figured maybe my mom would do better than that. It didn't turn out that way but **at first things were going pretty good.** I was living with hope and I kept that hope until I was nine, ten years old. **I was doing kid things,** going out, playing cowboys and Indians, running around with my cap gun, playing military, that type of thing. I got hooked up with different programs out there, like Wilderness Venture, which is an Outward Bound program. I would go out and do things.

Meanwhile at that time, my mother had various boyfriends that came in and out of the picture. I'm not trying to say my mom's a slut, but she just got around. She needed the support; she needed the companionship. But **she was a bad judge of character.**

Then my mother met someone I liked. **He was cool, a nice guy, always had money,** always took care of the family. If I needed something *he* was there for *me*. He was always there for me. **If I wanted to talk, he would listen.**

Granted **he was a drug dealer,** a really bad user for a bit; he was into heroin, coke, he was doing all kinds of things. For a while **when I was eight or nine I was carrying for him.** I carried little gram packets, grams of coke, grams of heroin. Grams of heroin are worth $400 to $500, but still, I'm carrying and he's not; he's walking me to the place and taking me home. He goes and collects the money; I just got to give it to the guy.

So I delivered his drugs. And at first it was all new to me. It was like I was being reborn. **I had a new family that I had never seen before;** I got the opportunity to make new friends. It was not what I was used to, because when I was younger, I was an outcast.

It made me feel important, trusted. And he was there for me. If I wanted to talk and he had a job to do, he'd tell them, "Listen, I got to talk to the kid." He'd leave his business to talk to me. I liked the guy. And **he'd give me money** — twenty bucks here, fifty bucks there. I was building model cars, plastic models; it was just enough to pay for that. Sometimes he'd buy one for me, little odds and ends to keep me happy.

But now I had a family — grandmother and grandfather. **I made him my father,** a father figure, because my mom had been going out with all these guys. He was a steady person: he was always there. **Sometimes he was kind,** but he was a diabetic, so his temper rose and fell every couple of days. It was pretty much unpredictable. **He tried to kill me once** — strangled me because I was in the back of the truck. He was driving; we were picking up my mother at the Seven Eleven. I was having a conversation with my sister and he was trying to tell me something and I told him to hang on a second while I finished my sentence. **He just snapped** and reached out and tried to kill me, strangle me. I had to wear turtlenecks for two weeks because **I had marks from his fingers.**

I DIDN'T WANT TO CARRY ON THE REST of my life the way that I was leading it. But though you can leave your past, your past never leaves you. You can quit the gang but they're not going to want you to quit. I wanted to change; I still do.

After that, though, he got arrested and sent away for ten years.

In middle school I just freaked. Even though the principal always tried to help me, I just didn't want to hear about it. Maybe he saw **something in my character that was better** than what I was able to get out.

But I started mixing with the gang-banger prospects, the future gang-bangers. They weren't there yet, but their brothers, cousins, fathers — **they were gang-bangers, and they were looking for recruits.** At the end of fifth grade you're about the right age; you start making the connection. Once you're in sixth grade, that's it.

I started being friends with people who... well...of course **some of them are dead now.** I'd say a good quarter of the kids were gang members. The other three quarters didn't really care – or they were the victims. There was such an epidemic in the school that **the principal banned certain gang-related colors:** black and yellow, blue and green. You couldn't wear bandannas that were blue; you couldn't wear sneakers that had black and yellow. There was a time where the kids wore beads, just regular beads, to show the colors: four beads together, yellow, black, yellow, black. There was a time when they banned those. **If you were caught, you would be suspended,** and there would be a big police investigation about why you were carrying those colors.

You don't really know what you're getting into when you're being courted by the gang. You have an idea, but you're looking at the money, you're looking at the jewelry, you're looking at the cars, you're looking at the girls, you're looking at the parties, you're looking at the fun, the family — **and it doesn't really matter if you die.**

> WITH GANGS, YOU BECOME a sheep. If they tell you to go beat up somebody to make an extra fifty bucks, you go and do it.

It's really hard to resist. When they go out on a recruiting binge, **they pick certain people,** the outcasts in the school, the ones who have more balls, that ones who get sent to detention more often than anybody else.

They don't pick the bad boys as recruits, bad guys who don't really care. **Not the bad boys,** because there are bad boys who are idiots, who just get into fights because they want to fight. The people they want are the people **in whose eyes you can see** what they'll be willing to join.

They choose the guys who look up to them, the ones who you can see have **a closet dream of being a gangster.** The kids who can't afford the good clothes, but they get the best they can and they try to keep them clean. **The kids who try to impress people,** try to make it look like they have money, like they have one twenty-dollar bill but underneath that they have a bunch of ones. The recruiters see that, and they figure, OK, **this kid wants to be something,** so let's go talk to him, let's test him to see if his loyalty is as strong as is he's trying to portray it.

Then **they give you these little jobs.** They'll say "This guy owes me $50." Then they send you out to collect and you come back and you give them the $50. You don't take $10 and tell them, "Oh all he had was $40." You give them the $50. If they send you out to buy something at the store, you get the receipt, you come back, you say, "here's your change and here's the receipt." **You have to show your loyalty,** that you're not going to steal from your own family, that's what you got to show.

So I arrived with hope but went from redneck to gang-banging.

Why did I do it? I don't really know. Maybe I just saw something in the gang that I didn't see in the house. **It was cool.** You were hanging out with all these kids. You're not allowed to own guns but everybody's got

Anonymous

them. **They're selling drugs,** getting all kinds of stuff, getting attention from girls, attention from local kids.

True, if you're **selling heroin to the little kids,** then other kids will come up and give you shit for it. You'll get a bad reputation for all kinds of stuff. If you're a gang that fights a lot, you get a reputation. If you can't defend your turf, you get a reputation for that. **People look down on you.** You become the punk, and you don't want to be that, so you have to be stronger than everyone else. You have to be able to work in a group. **You have to be able to follow their rules,** and you get respect for that.

It's not all innocent. **It's not all innocent.** We weren't. Sure, we had a lot of parties, and we got a lot of respect from the neighbourhood, but at the same time we were still selling guns, **we were still selling drugs,** we were still beating up people for their money, doing typical gang things, traveling into other gangs' neighborhoods and causing a ruckus.

But at the same time **you learn to trust these people more than your own parents.** You do the things that they want. You look up to the president. He tells you to do something, you got to do it, because you want him to think of you as a good soldier. **You want the respect of**

the council. If they tell you to go beat up somebody to make an extra fifty bucks, you go and do it.

That's one of the problems with gangs, **you become a sheep.**

Another problem is that, **of my old friends, a good forty per cent are dead** — and not of natural causes. Some took their own lives, some were killed in gang fights, some were shot, some **people were killed** because they didn't want to give up something they owned...

Suicide is not that rare, because **you can't get out.** There's no way out, once you're in. **Your only way out is to get killed or to kill yourself.** You can't leave, once you get tattooed or branded, one or the other, you can't really leave. If you try, **anything could happen.** You could have a fall in the bathtub, those things — things that look like accidents but aren't.

And **you never, never grow out of it**...at thirty-five, for example, you may want out, you may come to that point, but the gang will see you as knowing too much. You're a liability at that point. So the option is, **do you really want to buy it,** or do you want to just stay in the system and live with it, deal with it? Plus, don't forget, some of **those people are your family now;** you've done a lot of things with those people — you can't just leave.

Like there was a man in my crew who owned a bar with another member and he wanted to sell out. The partner didn't want to pay him. So one day he was coming home and closing the car door and **somebody came up with a nine-millimeter and just filled him full of lead,** turned him into a pencil. Next thing, they rolled him under the car in front of his family and kids and took off.

Still, **it's hard to resist.** Your own family is screwed up — you got an alcoholic mother, a drug-abusing father — then you go to school and you've got **all these kids who've got money, they've got love,** they show you respect, they're not beating you up everyday.

The worst thing I did would be the thing that got me sent back to Canada. I had to collect $50, and the guy didn't want to pay. So **me and my friend grabbed him and hung him outside a window by his ankles.** We told him, "you're going to pay or we're going to drop you." He paid. **I would've dropped him,** too. I don't doubt in my mind that I would have dropped him. I mean, if I don't do it, I'm going to get killed. Him or me, that's the choice, and I'm not in the mood to die.

I got arrested for that, so after that **I had to serve time.**

Peggy

And **they wanted me to rat on my people.** I wasn't going to when these were the guys who were paying for the things I couldn't afford, who were showing me more love than I got at home.

If you were to ask me, "did your mother beat you," I'd say, **"yes, my mother beats me every day."** But if you were to ask me, "do your friends beat you, your gang member friends," — no, **they never touched me in my life.** Even though they beat the hell out of me when I came in to the gang.

I got a beating then that I'll never forget.

I didn't want to carry **on the rest of my life** the way that I was leading it. But the thing is, you can leave your past but **your past never leaves you.** You can quit the gang but they're not going to want you to quit. When I decided **I wanted a different life,** I had to keep a gun for protection.

I wanted to change; I still do. The biggest obstacle is leaving your friends. It's hard to leave your friends to make new friends. And if you don't make new friends, you're alone. And **when you're alone it gives you time to think.** You get bored, and when you get bored, you think "I can do crime" and that's exciting. **And then you go outside and do crime,** break into a car, steal a car, do little stuff, it doesn't have to be anything major, like robbing people at the subway.

Also, **people still saw me as a gang-banger.** And I still had this idea that I was a gang-banger. So **they were scared of me** or they didn't like the way I was acting. They wanted to fight me and then **I had to protect myself** because I didn't feel confident enough that I could beat them up because **I was alone.** I didn't feel I had the proper backing, so I carried a gun...

Then more trouble....and **I ended up in Bordeaux for break and enter,** possession of weapons. I did two-thirds of my time. Now, I'm still part of their property, so if I screw up, I can still go back and do the last third of my time. **I'm on probation for ten years.**

The thing is, **I still have to look over my shoulder.** You can leave it, but it doesn't leave you. You rob somebody back when you're twenty and you're twenty-three and that guy is still looking for you. **People that you rob don't forget you robbed them.**

But I'm moving on. **I have job.** It's an agency where I wait with another thirty, forty people and then we get contracts and we're just sent out to work. It's mainly manual labor. They pick you out — you, you, you, you, go here — then you spend all day there, and it's **maybe ten dollars an hour, maybe twenty dollars an hour,** it depends on where you go. Then once you're done, you go home. And the next day you go back and you wait, and **every day it's a job.** I worked in a yogurt-packing place. I just packed boxes.

> You make friends, and you have a goal together; the group's goal to change our lives, and we all want to. We're all going through the same struggles, the same feelings.

By the end of the day, **I'm so tired I don't want to do anything.** I go home, I go to sleep, I sleep until seven in the morning and then I'm back out, till five thirty. You're doing work. **It fills my time,** by the end of the day I have maybe a couple of hours and it's just enough time where I can break down and just relax and read a book, go to sleep.

My hopes right now are just not to backslide.

I'm moving forward right now and I want to keep going.

I don't want to be a burden on anybody's back.

I just want to live.

L.O.V.E. changed a lot. It changed a lot of my life, helped me out a lot. It's a grounding point where I can look back and reflect because **before that, I didn't really think about my life.** I didn't really look back and think about what I'd done, where I was going with it. I didn't really want to change. It seemed all good to me: it's fine, I'm doing OK. Now that I hooked up with L.O.V.E., did some of the programs, did the schooling, did the book, talked about the life, it's like a clearing out.

You think about what you did, then you realize you're a real idiot, you could've done other things. **What were you thinking?** It's a release: you come here and you want to change. It's the only thing you can do when you come here. **You have to want to change.**

Groups like L.O.V.E. are just trying to make it safe. **There are a lot of people out there that don't feel safe.** If you can get little groups to work with other little groups and **spread the word** and get all those other little groups together, then it'll make the collective a lot stronger.

And the rest of the world will have to pay attention.

Yeah, that's one of the things about this place. I came here and I found people that were not like me, but they were outsiders. Then **you make friends with them, and you both have a goal,** and the whole group has a goal to change their lives, and they all want to. **They're all going through the same struggles,** the same feelings.

I want to help; **I'd like to help.** I'd like to use the insight that I have into what I went through. But the thing is that if people don't want to know about it, then they won't change. **You can only help others to change as much as they want to.**

Chapter 10

Sexual Abuse

In this chapter we hear the courageous voices of those who have experienced sexual abuse. They describe both the devastation it has wreaked in their lives, and their determination to recover and heal.

Anonymous, 15

To my stepfather:

I'm scared. I'm scared of you. **You hurt me.** You hurt my family. **I blame you for my pain.** I blame you for my sleepless nights, for my mother leaving me, for the tears that ran from eyes, for the tears I don't have left, for all the screaming that still echoes in my mind, for **all the nightmares. You took everything** and anything I had left. You made me want to take my life and **for all this I blame you,** stepfather.

Anonymous, 15

To my abuser,

Please stop. **I don't understand why you are touching me.** What did I do? Did I say anything or did I let it happen? Was it my fault? Did I make you do this to me? I now know **hiding does not help;** you find me and it starts all over again. Even now, I see you. **You're in my head.** I try to get you out. I want you out. Please get out and please stop.

I'M THE ONE

Anonymous, 18

I'm the one who remembers what it was like to be held down.
I'm the one who remembers what it was like to keep a secret.

I'm the one who went crazy — why wasn't it you?

Someday I'll have the guts to tell on you.

I'm the one who felt the pain of rejection. I'm the one who
can't have a relationship. I'm the one with funny hair and
weird piercings. I'm the only one and someday I'll have the
guts to tell on you.

Someday I'll tell on you.

Bronwyn

The Face in the Mirror

Anonymous, 15

I look into the mirror and see **someone I thought I knew.** I look deep into the eyes of a little girl who is lost in a world that she believes is reality. She is blinded by the lies that she lives. **She turns to drugs, alcohol and violence.** She believes there are no other roads to turn down.

She lived in a home where **secrets were not revealed,** not even to her own father. The home that was once happy turned into a living nightmare.

There was **a little girl who would come home scared,** knowing that her six foot, six inch stepfather was waiting with **a belt in his hand,** ready to bare her bottom and hit her till she could not scream or shed any tears.

She then knew that he was raping her oldest sister and **she could not say anything** in fear of losing her sister and her mother.

When this little girl turned into a teen, **the nightmare got worse.** She came home to that six foot, six inch man and he would fool around and touch her in places that she did not want touched. **Yet the secrets were not to be revealed to anyone.** She would say, "leave me alone," and yet the man would still pretend to tickle her. She was afraid of losing what her sister had lost.

The last day that she remained in that house sticks in her mind forever; **the image will not go away.** The man puts her on the floor. He pins her elbows with his knees and sits on her chest and gives her a smile. **She is on the floor and cannot get free from this man.** She believes and fears she will lose something to this man and tries to get free. The man hears someone coming up the stairs and jumps off.

She stayed at her father's house, **afraid to go back to the one she left.** She had to lie to her loved ones so she would not have to go back.

Then her father learned what happened behind those doors and the reason why she lied to him all those years. **Her father cried, knowing the pain she had gone through.**

When I look back into that same mirror, I can see the changes in the face staring back at me. The once scared little girl is now a woman, **a young woman who knows that violence is not the way** and that alcohol does not wash away your problems.

I am now a bright, funny girl who **can accomplish anything I put my mind to.** The young woman in the mirror is not perfect, but she's trying hard to be as perfect as she can be. I look into that mirror and **see someone who is still going through changes — changes for the better.**

HOW MUCH MORE COURAGE can you get than from seeing, hearing, feeling and living a life all about fear? Just living my life has taken courage.

Anonymous, 17

My best friend and I were inseparable. Since we lived on the same street, **we did everything together.** When I turned seven, she moved away from my street and so we could only play together on weekends.

I ended up sleeping over at her house almost every weekend. We did everything "normal" kids did. We watched TV, played with Barbies, and begged for brownies. The days at her house were great. **The nights were slowly tearing me apart.**

You see, my friend had an older brother. When I was five or six, **I thought he was great.** He played with us, took care of us, and even helped us make clothes for our dolls. **But something started changing.** He became more and more affectionate with me, more than he was with his sister.

I found myself **increasingly scared of him,** but I put my fears aside, thinking they were irrational. When he started coming into my room at night, I thought it was my fault. When he climbed into my bed and touched me, **I clenched my jaw and pretended to sleep.** If this was happening to me, it was obviously my fault. Something I had done was causing this to happen. Or maybe this was normal, and I was just over-reacting. Mum said I over-reacted a lot. **I could never bring myself to say anything** – I didn't want to get into trouble. I hated the sound of people yelling.

I LOOK INTO THAT MIRROR and see someone who is still going through changes — changes for the better.

I thought I let him do this. I thought I was supposed to. As I got older, five years later, **I couldn't take it any more.** My insides were crumbling away. I had lost so much to him — my sense of pride, my self-confidence, my self-awareness, and my best friend, because I stopped hanging out with her. It hurt so much to stop seeing her, **but it was the only way to save myself.**

If I could change anything about that part of my life, I would change the way it made me see myself. I felt useless to my guy friends if they didn't "want" me. Boyfriends were even worse. I couldn't stand them touching me; I couldn't stand them not trying to. Every guy I bumped into became a predator, something to be scared of. **I felt so completely alone.** I withdrew from all my friends.

But now I realize that he is the one that hurt me. **It was his fault.** He did this. And knowing this has allowed me to change. **I know I'm not useless.** I am allowed to be sexual on my own terms. I can learn to be strong again. He hurt me, but he didn't break me. **I'm going to feel this hurt every day;** I'm going to remember him every night. I'll feel him with every touch. **But I'm going to learn not to blame myself.** I'm going to learn to go forward with my life. I'm going to learn that my boyfriend's touch is not his. **I'm going to be strong again for me.**

Malcolm

Anonymous, 16

I don't know why I didn't **call the police** or even think of using any kind of force. I knocked on the locked bathroom door, trying to be as annoying as possible so that I could get inside or she could get out, but **I gave up too quickly.** Then I sat on my bed and talked and talked with other friends about the longest word in the English language **while my friend was being raped.** Maybe I didn't act upon the feeling that something horrible was happening behind that locked door because **the air was thick with the smell of weed and heavy with the taste of alcohol.** I had knocked on the door when I heard the bumps on the wall, but that was the extent of my inquiry into why my bathroom had been occupied for forty-five minutes straight. My friend came out of the bathroom with **red strangle marks on her neck.** I wish I hadn't taken such a laid-back approach while **she endured forty-five minutes of hell in my bathroom.** I didn't know exactly what had been happening, but I should have. When I look at my friend, I'm transported back to the **ripped shower curtain, the dented radiator and her tears.** How much she must have been hurting in that room, hearing her friends on the other side of the door **calling for her, then fading away.** Then I remember myself, sitting paralyzed on the bed with smoke-filled lungs and **not knowing what to do or say.**

NOW I REALIZE that he is the one that hurt me. It was his fault. He did this. And knowing this has allowed me to change.

Anonymous, 15

The day is finally near when **I will be walking through the doors of a courtroom.** I will need all the courage that has grown in me over the years to face my abuser, to look him straight in the eyes and tell him, "**I'm not scared any more. You don't control me; you can't.**"

I have feared this day. Thinking about it made me wonder if I would have the courage to do it. Then it hit me: of course I would. **I lived through abuse every day of my childhood.** How much more courage can you get than from seeing, hearing, feeling and living a life all about fear? **Just living my life has taken courage.**

I'm going to learn not to blame myself. I'm going to learn to go forward with my life. I'm going to be strong again for me.

Anonymous, 16

As the beer bottle came towards my face at full force, I was paralyzed with fear. The pain that had built up and been kept in for what felt like an eternity was released like the shattered pieces of glass that cut through my face. All that pain erupted within me like a volcano, and I snapped, becoming almost like him. With a fist strong as the impact of a hammer, I hit my best friend— my best friend who wanted to sleep with me, who refused to take "no" for an answer. "What the hell is going on?" I repeated in my mind, afraid of what would happen next. I didn't wait to see; I ran out of his life with pride and dignity.

Patricia

Anonymous, 15

Happiness is something I couldn't live without. My happiest moment would have to be the Christmas break of 1999. Every Tuesday of that year, I had a group meeting with other girls who had been sexually abused. Around the Christmas break, we all went to a restaurant and had a gift exchange. We talked and laughed, and for once **I was surrounded by people who understood my pain and my past.** The laughter and joy that filled the restaurant made me realize how far I have come from the things that happened so long ago.

One of the leaders in the group gave me a journal and wrote something that inspired me to be happy in the days to come. So **I filled the journal with pictures and little sentimental objects that I stuck on the pages.** Now, when I go back and read through my journal, **I feel good about myself** and good about who I've become.

Sally

Chapter 11

Intolerance

Looking beyond the surface of difference, these writers explore the damage that prejudice and racism can inflict.

Acid Shower

Ali, 15

The acid shower **washes all the hate and darkness off you**; it burns you on the inside and outside. While your old skin peels off, another layer is produced. Wash down your tears in the shower where **all the hatred is released;** some are still on you.

The next day **more hatred and darkness fall upon your new layer of skin.** Kids laughing at you and discriminating against you because of the way you look and dress. **That's the hatred coming your way.** Taking their laughter, taking the acid shower becomes a daily cycle for you.

Mohammed's Story

Mohammed immigrated to Canada from Afghanistan via Switzerland at the age of twelve. Now nineteen and enrolled in an art program at college, he looks back at the rough days.

I have tried to put my anger behind me, **but it keeps coming back.** I was angry at my parents for their lack of support. I was angry at myself because I was a loser, because I didn't have friends. I never hung out until I was fifteen or sixteen. **I was pretty lonely all the time** and I analyzed things too much. I wanted to be bigger and badder and worse, and I wanted to hang out with the tough crowd, but **I was not cool enough.**

The fact that I couldn't get friends killed me. When you don't have any, your self-esteem just drops and you get angry at yourself. A lot of it had to do with moving from culture to culture. **You are so lost,** because you're trying to figure out how you're supposed to behave around these people, what's wrong and what's right in this society, what's cool and what's not cool... When I first came here I mouthed off to a lot of people that I shouldn't have. But I was thinking, hey man, **I'm alone here.** I've got to protect myself.

And racism does not help it at all. I didn't know the language, so that didn't help. Your average kids, being totally ignorant, just perceive you

I WANT PEOPLE TO see me for me. I need to feel like an equal. I need my heart to heal.

based on what they've learned…I was called "Paki" a lot; I was called "ref", because I didn't know the language and I wasn't dressed the best. **The kids all put you down for what you look like and who you are.**

You can't catch up with your emotions and when you're a kid, you can't help yourself, because **you're confused and lonely.** I mostly blamed myself for my frustration. I took the easy road, I guess, and I also brought it upon my brother. **I left scars on my brother; actual scars on his face.**

For the past few years I tried to hide from my anger in drugs and that didn't work at all. **Drug use makes you even more depressed.** At first drugs do seem to make you happy and you concentrate on the positive stuff, but in the end it makes you more depressed. I began to realize that I had forgotten a lot of things. My memory was slowly fading away.

Now I'm working and going to college. I have responsibilities. It makes you feel like you're someone.

Zico

Anonymous, 15

The only way to stop violence is to open your mind and everyone's mind.

Anonymous, 16

Who grows from violence? Does it ever teach us a lesson that we couldn't have figured out in a peaceful way? **If we could just all open our minds,** if we could just learn to accept each other. **If we could just grow from each others' differences,** instead of finding them threatening and wasting our energy on hating each other...we could gain so much from everybody.

Sometimes I Feel Like Nothing

Sometimes I Feel Like Nothing

Anonymous, 16

I am nothing but a handful of dirt and rocks. **People step on me and I am crushed.** Broken, shattered and splintered. I am spat on and smeared. Occasionally, someone notices me and picks me up. They poke and prod, sift through me, through my heart, my soul and my feelings. **But they never find anything good** so they throw me into the wind. I land hard. Scattering everywhere. And I try to pick up my pieces.

I am nothing.

We're all human and we all deserve acceptance.

Anonymous, 11

You're playing in the park, when somebody starts squeezing your fingers against the metal of the monkey bars. You fall down and hurt your leg. You're surrounded by teenagers, all around sixteen years old.

One of the teenagers **kicks you as you try to get up.** The tallest one pulls out a knife. You ask what you did wrong. At first, they don't answer. Finally one of them says, "Go back to India!" You're not from India, you're from Guyana. You tell them where you're really from. A teenager with a dog says, "You're still shitty brown and you're playing on our monkey bars."

One of them **picks you up by the hair, and punches you on your side.** You know you have no way of winning. When he throws you down, you jump up and start to run. They let the dog loose, but **you make it home before they catch you.** Lucky you live close, or they would have pulverized you.

I'M NOT A JOKE. I'M A
PERSON WITH FEELINGS

Lindsay, 15

It happens all around the world **in different forms,** in different ways. We fear anything that is different, anything that is out of the ordinary. This fear is something we are born with, born into. It's a part of our past. It's part of our present day. **It will be a part of our future** unless we all decide to stop it.

Jeff, 18

WHEN I WAS FOURTEEN, **I was an angry and confused kid.** My whole life I had been beaten; from the age of twelve on I was doing drugs.

I joined a gang, but it wasn't a regular gang, **it was a racist movement.** Basically, we were a bunch of guys who got drunk and went out looking to fight. I didn't stick with them long. Within two months I had **stabbed a kid in the face with a broken beer bottle.** I'd come close to being put in jail numerous times.

I had become good friends with a Métis girl in my group home. **She was so beautiful and funny that no one could hate her.** It was the first time I realized that I liked a person for who they were. To make a long story short, she was my girlfriend for three years. **I learned a lot from her.**

Now that I live back in my old neighborhood, I'm one of the only white kids. Most of my friends are Black and you know what? **That's fine with me.**

PRIDE

Anonymous, 16

Savage, no!
Native, yes!
You can push me,
punch me — it won't change
who I am.
I don't care what you think.
I no longer feel bad, ashamed, afraid
of who I am.
I feel happy, glad and love
my race.
I am who I am
and if you don't like it, I'm okay with that
because I like who I am and
I like who you are, your race,
and I'm not going to be racist
to you because of how you treated me.
I'm Native
and proud!

JUDGING

Anonymous, 15

Why do you judge
everything you see move?
You judge.
Why?
I haven't done anything.
You don't even know me.
So why do you judge?
Don't you think about how I feel?
You don't use your head.
You don't think twice before speaking.
I do have feelings.
I do have a background.
I do have the past,
the present and the future.
You don't know me at all
and you judge.
Let's switch places
and tell me how you feel with me judging you.
So how do you feel?
Do you still want to judge me?
Yes or no?
This is me.
Take it or leave it but don't make fun of me because of it.

Not Cool Enough

Crystal, 15

If you're not cool or you don't hang out with the right group of people, you're considered an outcast, a nerd, a freak, etc. That can lead to frustration, which can then lead to depression and anger. That anger will then build up inside, and it has to come out in some way. And when a kid is driven to the breaking point, that's when the anger and violence comes out.

When you're not cool, the feelings inside of you are overflowing. You are filled with fear, depression and anger. **Fear comes first.** You fear going to school because you might be laughed at, embarrassed, or get your ass kicked.

Then comes depression. It's the thought that no one cares, that no one will be your friend and that feeling of sadness all the time. Then there is the anger, which you don't feel till the breaking point.

Other people don't know how it feels to be uncool or picked on. When someone tells them they don't know how it feels, they might say, "yes, I do know how it feels," but they really don't.

To help kids you should treat them with understanding, listen to them with an open mind, and provide comfort and support.

Anonymous, 15

People don't see me as anyone important. **I don't mean anything to anyone**. They put me down; my nicknames at school are freak, stupid, dumb, idiot, ugly, loser... Even my friends put me down. **I've always been picked on because of my differences.** But there's nothing wrong with me. I like being myself. I don't want to be like everyone else, like what society tells you to be. I'm my own person. What's wrong with some people is that they don't want to see that, they just want to point and judge. **Can't people see that that's just the way I am?** I wish I was accepted. But people don't care to see the real me.

I like my personality, but when **people call me a freak all the time**, I start believing it and calling myself that, like it's a joke. **I'm not a joke.** I'm a person with feelings. Maybe I'm too nice to people. But this is the way I am and it's up to other people to accept that. **I want people to look at me** and say, "I know that girl; she's cool" instead of saying, "Oh my God, that girl is such a loser." I wish society didn't judge others and that we all respected and accepted each other. We're all human and we all deserve acceptance. **Prejudiced people make fun of others for no good reason** — because they're fat, buck-toothed, wear glasses... I think that if you're prejudiced, it's because **you don't understand yourself** or anyone else. Why judge someone you don't even know?

Katie

Amber, 16

To help kids, you should **treat them with understanding**, listen to them with an open mind and provide comfort and support. **If someone had listened to me,** maybe I would feel less like a dumb, messed-up freak. **I'm going to listen to other people** and maybe one day, I will help someone. People should be seen and heard — not judged and hurt.

Jonathan

WHEN A KID IS DRIVEN to the breaking point, that's when the anger and violence comes out.

Chapter 12
Your Turn

IN THIS CHAPTER, we invite readers to join us in exploring youth culture by speaking out about their lives. Writing honestly about our experiences makes us think about them in a way we haven't before. Also, since **honest writing is powerful writing**, chances are that you will get great satisfaction from what you produce. If you've found the stories you've read in *The Courage to Change* inspiring, this is your opportunity to **pick up a pen, or reach for a keyboard,** and tell your own. The following writing assignments were used in the L.O.V.E. journalism programs which produced this book. Now it's your turn. **Do them just to do them,** or submit them to us for our coast-to-coast newspaper, *One L.O.V.E.*, written for youth by youth.

We also accept black-and-white photographs that express your feelings on these subjects. Our address is:

> 1015 Atwater
> Montréal, Québec
> Canada H3H 1X4.

Our email address is:

> Lovemtl@qc.aira.com

We have only **one rule** about writing for our books and newspapers. Since our goal is to give an accurate picture of the challenges faced by teens, **the stories must be true.**

All the photographs in this Chapter (except pages 155 & 161) by Maureen Rodriguez Labreche

CHAPTER 1 - EMOTIONS

- WRITE a letter to someone else (a friend or relative) who is feeling seriously depressed. **Share your ideas** on what you feel is important in life, on the things that you enjoy and that keep you going when you are feeling very low. **Be specific.** You can do it in list form if you like; try to make the list **as long as you can**. Can you reach twenty-five items? fifty? a hundred?

- WRITE the above letter to **yourself.**

CHAPTER 2 - SELF-IMAGE

- DESCRIBE the quality about yourself that you **most like** — it can be a physical characteristic or an aspect of your personality. **What is it** about that quality that you like so much? What else do you like about yourself? Try to make an entire list.

- PICK a friend, relative, or acquaintance who is **very different from you**. For example, if you are a **soft-spoken** person, pick someone who is more **aggressive**. Write about him or her. Would you want to be like this person? If yes, **why?** If no, **why not?**

CHAPTER 3 - HOME

- WRITE about someone in your family who has had **a strong effect** on you in either a negative or a positive way. It could be a younger brother who makes you feel important and protective, an **uncle or parent** who is hurtful, or a parent whose hard work and kindness inspires you. Describe this person in **detail**, including their physical appearance. Show them in a situation that **reveals their character.** Explain the effect this person has had on **your life, your ideas and behavior.** Do you want to be **like** this person? Do you want to be **different?**

CHAPTER 4 - DOMESTIC VIOLENCE

- WRITE an **open letter to the government,** your local youth services organization, or to society in general telling them **what you would do** if you had the power to make children safer in their own homes. Include in your letter a statement of **what the problem is, what is being done to solve it,** and **what should be done.** How would your ideas **change things** for abused young people? If you have had first-hand experience of domestic violence, **include a description** of your own experiences to demonstrate the importance of **your point of view** and to make your argument more compelling.

- WRITE down **the reasons** *you* think adults are **violent** towards children.

CHAPTER 5 - SCHOOL

- TAKE **a few brief notes** on the atmosphere you find at **your school** – in the halls, cafeteria, school yard. Detail snippets of conversation, **specific incidents**: how people look, what they do, how they treat each other. Gather lots of specific details. Then describe **your reaction** to the scene you've portrayed: Do you **love** school? **Hate** it? Feel something **in between?** Write your story focusing on the elements about your school that contribute to **how you feel** about it.

Anonymous

CHAPTER 6 - BULLYING

- IF YOU have **witnessed** or **experienced** an incident of **bullying** at your school or in your community, **take a moment** to write about it:

    Who was involved?

    When and **where** did it take place?

    How did it start and what happened?

    Has it been occurring on a **regular basis?**

    Were any **steps taken** to stop the bullying?

    What were the **results?**

    Why do you think the bully or bullies acted in **the way** that they did?

- IF YOU were the **head of the school board** in your area, what advice would you give to the **following people** about bullying?

    – teachers

    – parents

    – victims

    – bullies themselves

- HOW should we **respond** to bullies? What responses and consequences do you think are **fair?**

CHAPTER 7- DRUGS

- WRITE about someone whose involvement with **substance abuse** seriously affected his or her life. Describe the person's age, background, family history. **Talk** about the obstacles they faced in life and **why** drugs had such an appeal. **Describe** how this person got involved with drugs and the effect drug use had on their health, attitude, friends, family and education. Describe **your own response** to this person's experience.

CHAPTER 8 - RELATIONSHIPS

- DESCRIBE your **best friend**. Show **the qualities** that this person has that make him or her such a good friend. Discuss whether you have these **same qualities** yourself.

- WRITE about **what your expectations were of first love,** and then describe your experience of a **real** relationship.

- WRITE about **a fight you had with a friend,** then describe **how** you came to forgive each other and **continue** with the friendship.

CHAPTER 9 - GANGS

- WRITE about **why** someone might find gang life attractive.

- MAKE a list of **the things about your life** that can help you **resist** joining a gang .

- DESCRIBE **how you can help someone** who feels outcast, rejected, not respected; how you can keep someone from feeling they have **no connection to others.**

Do them just
to do them

write

CHAPTER 10 - SEXUAL ABUSE

- IF YOU yourself have experienced sexual abuse, **write a letter to your abuser** expressing your anger and your fear, and asking the questions **that you need answers to.**

- IF YOU have not spoken about the abuse yet, think about **who you would like to confide in.** Write about **why** you would pick this person, **what** you would say, and **how** you would want this person to react.

- IMAGINE yourself **ten years from now.** Describe the person you've become, how you look, how you feel, **what you have accomplished.**

CHAPTER 11 - TOLERANCE

- DESCRIBE a time when you were **quick to judge** someone by the way they looked, talked or behaved. Did you say anything **out loud** or did you keep your opinions to yourself? Where do you think your views come from: **family? community? the media? your own experiences?** When you think about it now, **how do you feel** about the way you reacted?

- WRITE about **someone you know** who is tolerant of others, regardless of their background, appearance or nationality; **someone who accepts people for who they are.** Describe how you **feel** when you're with that person.

Joy Futerman

Chapter 13

And here's what the adults say...

This book has depended on the wisdom and eloquence of our young writers to discuss topics that are central to their lives. In this chapter, we offer a few brief words from an adult perspective.

Feelings

Feelings

DURING ADOLESCENCE, life can feel like a wild ride, with **a broad range of feelings** and emotions being experienced in a short period of time. A mix of feelings — happiness, sadness, rejection, isolation — can bounce off one another all at the same time. Depending on what else is going on in their lives, **individuals respond in varied ways,** sometimes with violence, lashing out at friends, family or strangers.

While there is often an inclination to **deal with emotions privately,** because of the potential pain and embarrassment that disclosure can present, isolation can multiply the problems. Expressing emotions with a **trusted confidant** is not only a good idea, it is **a very courageous act.**

Self-Image

Self-Image

YOUNG PEOPLE entering their teenage years are exposed to **new thoughts, images and ideas** at the same time as their bodies are transforming themselves. They become aware of societal values and wonder **where they fit in** and how they are seen by the rest of the world. They feel pulled in a thousand directions, uncertain as to what to believe and confused about how they perceive themselves.

It is particularly important for young people to be assured that **individuals are all different,** that there is no one ideal of beauty. They need to be encouraged to recognize **their personal strengths** and build from them as best they can while being kind to themselves. **Compassion is the key.**

Home

Home

FEELING ABANDONED by one's own parents is a **profound and central betrayal** in young lives. The message that they are **not good enough** is corrosive to their development and growth. The tendency is for young people to **blame themselves;** they conclude that something is wrong with them, that they must have done something to make their parents reject, ignore or misunderstand them. There must be something wrong with them that precipitates **dad's anger,** makes mom drink or seek a divorce.

Under these circumstances, young people need reassurance that the family issues are **not their fault** and that **self-blame is no solution**.

Domestic Violence

Domestic Violence

ABUSE CAN HAVE many different effects, but the common thread is the development of low self-esteem and **a difficulty in developing healthy, trusting relationships** as adults. When a child experiences abuse from his or her primary caregivers, the effects can be long-lasting.

The victim of domestic abuse **must tell someone.** While the abuse often occurs within the privacy of the home, **domestic violence is not a personal responsibility**; it is one for which all of society is responsible. Today, lawmakers and government leaders have come to realize that it is everyone's legal and moral duty to report any suspected abuse of children. If the victim remains isolated, and the violence is not named or identified, help cannot be provided. **We must speak out.**

School

FOR ADOLESCENTS, school is not merely the place where teachers and parents want them to get an education, it is an important arena where they act out **the daily concerns and joys of being young.** But when the expectations of the young person's social milieu **conflict with the work of schooling and learning,** problems arise. The challenge is to **create a comfortable balance** between the social and educational parts of school. Although working out the specifics **may require assistance from a parent or professional,** in the long term the effort is worthwhile.

Bullying

WE HAVE COME TO LEARN that bullying is **not simply a "normal" part of growing up.** Recently, the news is full of tragedies where former victims of bullying have turned on those around them. The majority of **those who bully have been bullied** themselves. Too often, the cycle begins with a victim who ends up as a victimizer.

The reasons for this cycle are not difficult to understand. Besides the physical pain, victims experience a whole range of destructive feelings: **anger, fear, powerlessness, embarrassment and guilt.** In extreme cases, victims of bullying can become depressed, develop eating and anxiety disorders.

It is clear that **both young people and adults,** including parents and educators, must confront rather than tolerate bullying.

Drugs

Drugs

DRUG USE is linked with other difficulties in adolescent life. Taking drugs is often used to **deal with the emotional pain and suffering** young people experience in relationships, at school or at home.

However, using drugs will, on the contrary, amplify existing problems or create new ones. Rather than treating drug use in isolation, it is important to **identify the complex issues** with which a young person is struggling, and attempt to find alternatives that address them.

Relationships

Relationships

WHEN THE STRONG and supportive bonds adolescents have formed with others weaken and break, **the sense of disappointment and betrayal** can be overwhelming. Adolescents will tend to question their own self-worth if a relationship fails. It is important to affirm to young people that **healthy relationships are not about dependency;** they do not involve the need for perfection, nor are they about power, control or manipulation.

Gangs

IT'S NOT DIFFICULT to understand why young people who feel isolated, weak and insecure are attracted to gangs. **Gangs can seem to provide a kind of home,** a sense of belonging where young people believe themselves to be loved and respected. Within the gang, the individual can believe he or she feels stronger, no longer a victim.

However, within gang culture, **individual identity is lost.** Members find the need to prove themselves continuously. Friendship and security within the gang is tied to **towing the line.** Those who attempt to disengage from membership face violence, threats and intimidation.

Sexual Abuse

UNTIL RECENTLY, it was very difficult for victims to come forward about their abuse. **Society tended to ignore or diminish the problem.** There was also the tendency to make the victims feel that they have somehow contributed to the assault. The fact that **the abuser is commonly a family member,** friend or neighbor further complicates the situation. However, victims can now be assured that they are never at fault; that sexual harassment, rape (including date rape) and sexual abuse is always a wrong committed by the perpetrator. Sexual abuse is society's problem as well as the victim's. The victim must be helped to deal with the problems of trust, self-blame, fear, anxiety, powerlessness, and sometimes self-destruction, which sexual abuse can engender. **With support, the victim can become a secure, safe survivor.**

Intolerance

Intolerance

IT MAY BE DIFFICULT for adolescents to understand that intolerance is **not simply a product of an individual's attitudes and behaviors, but a reflection of a society** in which some groups have been granted more power, privileges and freedoms than others. Historically, prejudices and intolerance have focused on **race, religion** and **ethnicity**. But the list of stereotypes and prejudices also relate to disability, gender and sexual orientation.

Adolescents need models of adult behaviour which demonstrate that **discrimination is not only wrong, but socially unacceptable;** that people's appearance or belief system does not make them more or less valuable as individuals, or as members of our society.

ACKNOWLEDGMENTS

THANKS FOR THIS WONDERFUL BOOK go first to our talented and courageous youth authors and photographers. Next, to my co-founder of the L.O.V.E. programs, the devoted educator Stan Chase. Of course I want to thank our great team, including Maureen Rodriguez Labreche, Alyssa Kuzmarov, Joel Silverstein and Eric Mailloux (Montréal); Joy Futerman, Jessica Weiser, Buffy Childerhose, David Green, RonniLyn Pustil (Toronto); Carol Cross, Lisa Glanville, Jaynus O'Donnell, Nancy Kivisto, Karen Tulchinsky, Martin Hauck (Vancouver); Sarah MacLaren, Drew Yamada, Christine Orescovitch, Merrill Lyons, Alastair Duncan, Brownwen Trim, Enid Schaller, Chris Melanson (Halifax).

I want to give credit to Kelly di Dominico, who assisted me enormously in the compilation of this book. Finally, thanks to editor Rhea Tregebov, designer Stephanie Martin, and to Second Story's Margie Wolfe, for adding their talent (and patience) to this challenging task.

Brenda Zosky Proulx

CONTRIBUTORS' NOTES

Because of the sensitive nature of the subject matter in this book, some of our contributors have chosen to publish their writing anonymously. We salute their courage, and that of all of our contributors. We are proud of every one of them. We have chosen, however, to present all of the written contributions in this book using first names only, in order to protect the privacy of these young people.

Please note that for the most part, the ages indicated are the ages at which the contributors began to work on this book. Note also that L.O.V.E. youth photographers are credited by first name only.

ALEX A. has produced a large body of photographic work which can be seen in L.O.V.E.'s traveling exhibit.

ALEX B. was an active member and an inspirational leader of L.O.V.E. for a year.

ALEXIA, a candid speaker, has a strong writing style which allows her to share her stories with others..

ALI is a committed member of L.O.V.E. and a bold writer.

AMBER has been a member of the Halifax branch of L.O.V.E. for a year and is an impressive presenter as well as writer.

ANDREW has been an inspiring classroom presenter for the past two years.

ANGELA is a compelling writer who has never missed a journalism class.

BETH has been with L.O.V.E. for two years and has produced an exceptional body of work.

BRYAN writes forcefully about how the cycle of violence can poison a life, and about how it can be ended.

CRYSTAL's honesty and courage have made her an outstanding leader of the nonviolence movement.

DANIEL A. is a courageous writer and willing learner.

DANIEL B. is a powerful force in L.O.V.E., and an honest and mature writer.

FERDOUSI's dignified and graceful writing sets a remarkable example for other young women.

GARY's thought-provoking writing and personal courage make him an outstanding role model.

GEOFFREY has found sharing his stories and creativity with others an effective way to cope with stress.

JEFF has been a member of L.O.V.E. for three years. Although he was once living on the streets, he is now back in school, living at home, working part-time, and making a huge difference at L.O.V.E.

JEREMY has made an exceptional contribution to L.O.V.E. He is also a talented writer and photographer.

JESSICA is now studying to become a professional photographer. She is a talented leader in our elementary school programs.

JONATHAN is now a leader who inspires classrooms of elementary school children.

KATIE, who joined L.O.V.E. a year ago, is an enthusiastic and energetic writer.

KIMBERLY'S mature and original writing and strong personal presence allow her to effectively share her wisdom with the L.O.V.E. youth.

KYM is a talented writer whose courage and honesty are exceptional.

LAURA is a gifted and generous writer.

LINDSAY has been a committed member of L.O.V.E. for almost three years. She currently works for L.O.V.E. as a part of her cooperative education program at school.

MOHAMMED, one of the first youth members of L.O.V.E., has worked part-time as a L.O.V.E. staff member. He continues to be a powerful anti-drug abuse and anti-racism advocate.

MORGAN is a talented writer and articulate speaker who has made a tremendous contribution to the L.O.V.E. program.

PAT has proven himself an asset to L.O.V.E. who can be counted on to set a positive example.

ROXANNE, who has been with L.O.V.E. for a year, has become an integral part of the organization. Her commitment to social change is an inspiration to others.

SANDRA was involved with L.O.V.E. for a little over a year and in that time made an outstanding contribution to a documentary film about the organization. She is now out in her community working for change.

SAVANNAH's insightful writing encourages and inspires others at L.O.V.E. and in the community.

SHEENA is now a youth leader for L.O.V.E. who is committed to making a difference in the world.

STACEY was with L.O.V.E. for one year and in that time she became a skillful and confident writer and photographer whose dedication is apparent in her work.

SUZY is a writer who believes in the transformative power of creativity.

TIFFANY A. is an enthusiastic, outspoken and determined writer.

TIFFANY B. writes candidly about difficult issues; her insightful writing has affected the lives of many.

TOMZINE is an outspoken leader whose verbal and written presentations are focused and powerful. She is a peer mediator as well as educator.

VALERIE has been a resourceful L.O.V.E. member for over three years. Her integrity as a writer has been an inspiration to many others.

VICKI's thought-provoking, sensitive work shows a special talent for capturing emotions both in the subjects she photographs and in her writing.

Leave Out ViolencE
honours our community supporters

NATIONAL PARTNERS

CTV, a division of Bell Globemedia
Government of Canada, Strategy on Community Safety and Crime Prevention
Millennium Bureau of Canada
The Adolph & Klara Brettler Foundation, Mintz & Partners
The Ontario Trillium Foundation
Whitecap Venture Partners, Diamond Family

DIAMOND

The Chawkers Foundation
Canadien National
KPMG LLP
Miles S. Nadal, MDC Corporation
Jason & Heather Smith
TD Securities
UBS Bunting Warburg
United Way of Greater Toronto

PLATINUM

The Edward Bronfman Family Foundation
Harry L. Hopmeyer
Multiculturalism, Canadian Heritage
Molson Indy Festival Foundation
The Rotary Club of Toronto
Twinkle Rudberg
Vancouver Foundation
The Zeller Family Foundation

GOLD

Anonymous Donor •The John Baker Fellowes Family Foundation •Bank of Montreal
Samuel & Saidye Bronfman Family Foundation
•City of Toronto, Breaking The Cycle of Violence •Satoko Ingram

On behalf of L.O.V.E.'s youth, we wish to thank those who have
donated their time and resources in the belief
that the future of our youth is everyone's responsibility.